SOULS DON'T LIE

Jenny Smedley

Winchester, UK
Washington, USA)

First published by O Books, 2007
O Books is an imprint of John Hunt Publishing Ltd., The Bothy, Deershot Lodge, Park Lane,
Ropley, Hants, SO24 0BE, UK
office1@o-books.net
www.o-books.net

Distribution in:

UK and Europe
Orca Book Services
orders@orcabookservices.co.uk
Tel: 01202 665432 Fax: 01202 666219 Int. code (44)

USA and Canada
NBN
custserv@nbnbooks.com
Tel: 1 800 462 6420 Fax: 1 800 338 4550

Australia and New Zealand
Brumby Books
sales@brumbybooks.com
Tel: 61 3 9761 5535 Fax: 61 3 9761 7095

Singapore
STP
davidbuckland@tlp.com.sg
Tel: 65 6276 Fax: 65 6276 7119

South Africa
Alternative Books
altbook@peterhyde.co.za
Tel: 021 447 5300 Fax: 021 447 1430

Design: Stuart Davies

ISBN-13: 978 1 905047 83 3
ISBN-10: 1 905047 83 5

A CIP catalogue record for this book is available from the British Library.

Printed in the UK by Ashford Press

SOULS DON'T LIE

Jenny Smedley

BOOKS

Winchester, UK
Washington, USA

ACKNOWLEDGEMENTS

The conscious mind can refuse to accept the truth.
It can hide the truth from itself and from others.
The soul knows all.
The soul cannot lie.
Souls *don't* lie.
Jenny Smedley

Your vision will become clear only when you look into your heart.
Who looks outside, dreams.
Who looks inside, awakens.
Where love rules, there is no will to power; and where power pre-
dominates, there love is lacking. The one is the shadow of the
other....
Carl Jung

CONTENTS

DEDICATIONS

This book is dedicated to my husband Tony.

My soulmate, my friend, and the best person I have ever known.

CHAPTER ONE

My life fell apart in 1995. The collapse had started years previously, with recurrent nightmares, although at that time I didn't connect them with what was to come later. They were very vivid and too real, and the dire emotions I felt during the nightmares stayed with me, even when I was awake. One of them involved a rape, and for years I lived in fear that it was a premonition, something that was going to happen to me one day. At the time I had no idea why I was having the nightmare. The other one I had was about me committing suicide and as I was a person who had suffered from depression on and off since puberty, the scenario was only too possible. It never occurred to me that my nightmares could have anything to do with a past life. Like most people, past lives were something I joked lightly about, saying things like, 'I don't know what I did in a past life to deserve this!' It never occurred to me that my own subconscious was causing me to have the nightmares in an attempt to 'wake me up' to who I really was, and who I had really been.

I wouldn't have completely dismissed the idea of having past lives though. I was open-minded on spirituality. I had been brought up as a Catholic and become disenchanted with various aspects and dogma of the church, but I still believed that there was some sort of creator, some sort of order to the apparent chaos of the Universe and our everyday lives. I leaned towards the idea of the Universe itself being intelligent. My need to have some evidence that I was right, and that we weren't just spinning carelessly around on this ball we call Earth in a pointless race towards old age and death, was part of the reason I was depressed. I wanted to *know* that there was an end game.

Each depression took me deeper, and I had to expend more effort every time to bring myself back up. Why was I depressed? I had no idea. I had my wonderful husband, Tony, and Phillip, a great son. I owned the horses that I'd always wanted, and we kept them at home on our own small farm. Tony was my best friend, my lover, and my soulmate, and at the time I was under the impression that we only ever had one soulmate. So, I should have been ecstatic, but every time I came close to being happy, a big dark cloud would pop into my consciousness, but frustratingly, it would refuse to fully declare itself. Far from considering the nightmares as clues to the reason for this, I just thought them to be another reason to be depressed.

My thoughts and phraseology were very strange during the nightmares, and yet at the time they seemed perfectly natural, as did my strange dress...

I'm walking through dense and thickly canopied woodland. Although the sun shines high above, it's dark and mysteriously shadowed under the parasol of trees, and I can't see too far ahead. I'm dressed in a long blue gown that brushes the tops of my shoes, which are shiny and black, with silver buckles. The dress has a lace collar, which is folded back and lies across my shoulders. The silky blue material fits snugly around my waist and then falls gently across the curves of my hips and down almost to the ground. My hair is blond and curly, upswept in a delicate net.

I follow a narrow pathway, pushing my way between the leaf fronds that have grown across the path; sprays of green lace, highlighted by little shafts of dusty sunlight that wend their way through the foliage. I'm going to meet someone, and he will be surprised to see me so far from the house. I feel my lips curve into a mischievous smile as I anticipate his pleasure at my unexpected appearance. The woods around me seem serene and safe, despite the dim light, because that is my mood.

But my reverie is suddenly shattered when I hear a noise behind me, the sharp snap of a twig. I freeze and listen, and for a spilt second there's the rustle of something following me. I look over my shoulder, but I can't see anything. The thick and beautiful growth of greenery has suddenly become an impenetrable passage that has closed behind me, and I can't see through it. I walk on. Then I hear the noise again; some living thing is moving stealthily behind me, I'm sure of it. The woods that had a moment ago seemed familiar have suddenly become alien and dangerous. The feeling of peace is now a terrifying isolation.

My heart beats faster as fear touches my spine with icy fingers, making my shoulders cringe. I hurry on. Perhaps it's just my imagination, or a wild boar grubbing for food. Safety isn't too far away. Ryan is working just beyond the tree line, and soon I'll be able to call out to him. Then I hear the noises again, coming closer, and I'm certain someone, not something, is stalking me. The sounds are still muffled and indistinct, but I experience the terror a hunted animal must feel. I'm finding it harder to draw my breath; my chest feels tight, even though my lungs are demanding more and more air.

I pause briefly, uncertain of what to do, and the noise from behind stops, but I know there's somebody there. My heart flutters like a caged bird. I'm tempted to scream, so that Ryan will hear me and come to my rescue, but the man behind me would also hear, and knowing that I'm alerted to him, he might attack me sooner. If he thinks I remain unaware, it might stay his hand. Ahead, the trees start to thin out, and as they do, I think to myself, oh thank God, at last! I know that Ryan is near, and as soon as I reach him I'll be safe. I start walking again and quicken my pace a little. I still can't decide, now that I am so close, should I scream?

Suddenly all my choices are gone. A hand grips my gown from behind and a second hand grasps my hair. I'm pulled over backwards, and before I can make any sound apart from a sharp cry of shock, the hand clutching my gown lets go, and clamps over my mouth instead. When I hit the ground the wind is knocked from me, leaving me no breath to scream with. The treetops whirl above me as I tumble to the ground. I gasp for air as my attacker launches himself bodily on top of me. Then, there he is, the man who's been hunting me down. He looms over me. He's disgusting. He has long greasy hair that hangs in rattails around his face, which is grimy and sweaty. He plummets down onto my body, pinning me to the ground. Up close I can see his pale, icy, blue eyes, the whites of which are an unhealthy yellow as they bulge in animal frenzy against his purplish complexion, and I can see coarse veins standing out on his brow. The stubble of his unshaven beard folds into creases in the valleys of his pockmarked skin. I'm sickened, both by the obvious threat and by his close proximity to me. His face above mine is red and fevered as his bestial cravings drive him. His breath smells noxious with stale beer as it whistles between his broken and blackened teeth.

He holds my head pinned to the ground with his grip on my hair, and now he grabs my right hand. My left hand is still free. I start to hit at him with it, but my blows are feeble and weak with dread. He dodges my blows easily, his breathing fast and frantic. He lets go of my hair, using his body weight to hold me down, and with total horror I feel him begin to scrabble at my skirt. I twist and fight, but

I'm not strong enough. I convulse with abhorrence and try to scream, but a tortured whisper is all that I can form, "Ryan..."

My hands thrash, trying to push him away. He drags up my skirt, and my muscles grow weaker yet with fear. I feel his fingernails scrabbling at my bare legs; I feel his knees squeezing between mine with irresistible strength, and I want to die.

Then I hear a voice cry out in the distance, "Madeleine!"

The very sound of the voice galvanises me. It's Ryan! My power returns on a wave of elation and I claw at the man's face. Blood streams from his forehead, and he hesitates. I find my voice and scream as loudly as I can, "Ryan! Ryan! Help me!"

I would wake up instantly at that point, the name *"Ryan"* still on my lips, and echoing in my mind. I would feel hands on my shoulders and scream soundlessly, before I realised that it was only Tony holding onto me. I would fall into his arms, crying with relief, and curl instinctively into a ball, with my knees clamped tightly together. I would still be able to feel the places where the rapist's knees had been forcing their way between mine. I could feel the little scratches his fingernails had made on the insides of my thighs. It was disgusting. I'd be hot and sweaty, and I'd feel violated.

Tony and I often discussed the nightmare and the fact that in it this *Ryan*, whoever he was, was calling *me* Madeleine. It didn't make any sense.

"Who *are* they?" I often asked, but I was still no nearer to an answer. Neither of us had any idea who Ryan was, or why he featured so heavily in my recurrent nightmares. There was another question that really scared me, was that other man someone who was really going to rape me, or try to, one day?

Tony was always sensible about it, but he was worried, both about the nightmare and my depression. I didn't even dare tell him about the one where I'd killed myself! In that one I was walking through a period house, and following what appeared to be the ghost of a man, I jumped off the roof.

CHAPTER TWO

I was worried too. Over the last few months the darkness in my mind had become terrifying in its intensity and frequency, like it was building to a crisis point.

Most mornings I struggled to find a reason to get out of bed. I couldn't raise any enthusiasm about anything. My life seemed futile and overshadowed. I felt like I didn't belong anywhere, and that a part of me was missing. There was something I was meant to be doing, but search as I might, I could never find out what it was. I tried so many things to fill the void within me, hobbies, part-time jobs, collecting things. Nothing even came close to making me feel fulfilled. I was honestly beginning to wonder if it was all worth it. It was crazy. Tony and I had been together since I was seventeen, twenty eight years, and I'd never wanted anyone else, and that wasn't the problem. I apparently had the perfect life. But still, there was a constant background sadness, which occasionally welled up, and I was getting very afraid that one day soon it would overwhelm me altogether; I'd drown in it and never be able to come back.

I was stalked through the woods in my dreams and was about to be raped. My only hope was that I'd be saved by the mysterious *Ryan*. I had no idea who he was, and the dream never went far enough for me to see him. I felt that somehow, this stranger had the answer to my depression, as well as my nightmare. I just knew that the two things were linked. But I had no idea how I could find out if that was true. And why in the nightmare was I wearing such old fashioned clothes? I'd even gone so far as to look them up in an historical costume book. They seemed to be from the 17th century.

I was also suffering from a debilitating and pretty constant pain, low down in my left side. This was connected to the nightmares too, I just knew it, but I had no answers as to the reason for that either. It was all gradually stealing my soul. I could feel it seeping away with my courage. Surely no mere 'dream' could have such a draining effect? I admit it occasionally crossed my mind that maybe I was becoming mentally ill – it was one possible answer anyway.

A couple of days later I came very close to being convinced that I was indeed going insane. I was walking through the local shopping mall. I felt downhearted, and totally cut off from the other shoppers bustling around in their everyday lives. They all looked content, if not actually happy, whilst I felt…how I always felt lately…alone and somehow out of place, and consumed with anxiety. How could life go on for everyone else, uninterrupted around me, when I felt as if it was futile? Why couldn't I feel contented like them?

I looked into the shop windows but didn't really see anything. I didn't want to buy anything anyway, so what was the point? I remember passing a record shop and hearing a snippet of a song wafting out of the doorway. It meant nothing to me at the time…*if I'd only known how the King would fall, then who's to say, you know I might have changed it all…* were the words I heard. I hummed along to the tune under my breath – even though I'd never heard it before; it was catchy. It was months later before I recognised that this song had been another clue as to what was going on.

The next shop was a butcher's. I tried not to look. Tony and I were vegetarians and I hated the sight of dead animals, even when they were sliced up into neat sanitised chunks, so that people could kid themselves they were eating something other than a dismembered corpse. Butchers' shops were nothing but charnel houses to me. But for some reason my eyes swivelled involuntarily to look through the window, and I was compelled to see. Thunk! It was grim. The butcher slammed his cleaver into a side of beef. My eyes focused sharply on the red meat and the blood. As the sound of metal hitting flesh punched into my consciousness, a vision flashed in front of my eyes, shocking in its suddenness and brutality.

I fell into a waking nightmare as I was transported into another world. The thud of the meat cleaver was exchanged instantly for the thrust of a sword as it plunged sickeningly into flesh. The victim of the blade was a man I could see lying in some long grass, which had taken the place of the paved walkway. A fearsome kilted warrior, who yelled triumphantly as he struck, wielded the sword. I caught peripheral glimpses of more warriors, and a small band of terrified men dressed in peasants' clothes, under attack from them. The wounded man at my feet stared at me. His sharp blue eyes pierced my heart. He reached out...

Then, just as suddenly, the vision was gone again, and I was staring transfixed at the meat and the cleaver in the butcher's shop. I staggered, nausea rising in my throat. I turned away from the sight and leaned breathlessly against the window with my back to the shop.

Just in time to avoid any well-meaning Samaritans from asking me awkward questions, I managed to pull myself together enough to walk on. My mind reeled, petrified, *Oh my God! What was happening to me?* I had never been so scared in my life. I made my way along the shop fronts, feeling my way, as if I was under water. I was drowning in emotion.

I went home, not looking in any more windows, keeping my eyes on the ground. I didn't tell Tony what had happened; I was worried about the effect it would have on him. He was already stressed out to an almost lethal degree by his job. He didn't need a neurotic wife hanging like a millstone around his neck. It could be the last straw, the thing that dragged him under too. I felt like I was standing at the bottom of a deep dark pit, looking up and praying that something or someone would pull me out. I went to bed that night totally dispirited, but trying hard to hide it.

The next morning I stayed in bed, hunched up under the covers, for as long as I could. I was trying to hide from the world. Maybe I could, but I couldn't hide from my own mind. It twisted and turned inside my head like an angry rattlesnake. I finally managed to get myself out of bed at about eleven. I couldn't be bothered to get dressed though because I just had no energy. Lately I couldn't be bothered with anything relating to appearance. It just didn't seem to matter. I'd gained about three stones (45lb) in weight, and I hadn't had my hair cut for months. Make up? Oh no....not me. Who cared what I looked like?

Two thirty that afternoon found me sitting alone on the sofa, my fluffy dressing gown wrapped around me. Small comfort. Staring up at me from the coffee table was a bottle of sleeping pills. It was a way out. I couldn't see another one. I could see no future; just a steep downhill slide that looked too easy to slip down. Maybe I should do my family a favour and check out. Stop the world and get off. Then *it* would all be over. But what was *it?* If anything was going to stop me from taking the pills, it would probably be curiosity.

The pain was much worse too. It was there, as usual, nestling down in my left hand-side, reasonably quiet at that moment, but always ready to flare into an unbearable hot iron. Doctors had no idea what it was, and what it *could* be was just one more thing to worry about in the deep dark hours before the dawn. I looked at the pills, and they looked right back. I knew that Tony and our son would be devastated if I did it, but they'd have a chance to build a new life without my misery hanging on their spirits. I'd be doing it for them. Wouldn't I?

I was lying to myself because I knew that Tony would never get over it if I left him. He loved me as much as I loved him. We'd met when I was seventeen and married two years later, when he was twenty-one. This was a big part of the mystery that surrounded me. We were a storybook romance, so why was I now teetering this close to the edge? I had to find a bit of backbone from somewhere and carry on. If I swallowed those pills, I'd be doing it for me not him! The pills beckoned. The bottle was all I could see. It called out to me. I closed my eyes tight, scrunching them up, denying what I was contemplating. I opened my eyes wide and determinedly I slapped at the bottle, "No!" I told it. The bottle bounced off the table, scattering pills, which smattered against the TV screen.

Just at that very second, I got my first ever verbal message from what I came to know much later as my past life angel. This voice in my head, a message relayed from God said, "Switch on the TV." Not exactly the sort of message I would have expected. But I was so low that I was ready to snatch at any straw and at least the TV would distract me from self-destruction. I reached out and flicked the switch, and my mechanical companion shimmered into life. That was when it happened. And it changed everything. I'd never believed it before when I'd heard people say that their lives had changed in a single second. But I wouldn't ever doubt it again.

As the screen steadied, a man appeared in close up. I'd never seen him before. Then, inexplicably, although the screen flashed, the picture remained stuck. Something very odd was going on. Time stood still for the TV, or for me. My attention was being drawn to this stranger's face. I leaned forward and peered into the man's eyes. They were an unusually clear and crystalline blue, and they dominated his face. Something hovered at the edge of my mind. The screen was showing a preview for a concert, and I knew I had to sit and watch it. Just before my mind was able to grasp the significance of the man's eyes, time unstuck, the preview faded from the screen, and I sat gasping for breath. Something incredible had happened to me, and it was still happening. I felt poised on a knife-edge, standing at the edge of a cliff of revelation. Fall or jump, one way or another I was going to find out something amazing.

I waited for the concert to come on. Minutes seemed like days, for I knew my life hung by a thread, dangling, frozen, until I saw that face again and knew what it meant to me. Finally, the concert came on, and I did watch it, and when his face came into close-up I found myself whispering on a deep indrawn breath, "Oh my God," not really knowing why I'd said it, and then even more peculiarly I said, incredulously, "It's you…" I felt a big smile forming on my face, but at the same time, tears were streaming down it. I was feeling a rainbow of emotions, and then something I hadn't known for a long time; pure, unadulterated joy. I was uplifted. I had no idea why, but even then I knew that somehow the reason for my depression had been whisked away as if it had never existed.

Almost feverish with excitement I grabbed the daily paper, tore it open on the TV listings pages, and ran my finger down the schedule, to find out more about this mystery man was. It only said…*2.30pm A Country Music Treat as BBC 2 covers the Garth Brooks' concert from the Texas Stadium.* I dropped onto the sofa, and rocked back, the paper still clutched in my hands, "Garth Brooks?" I mouthed. Who? Why? All I had were questions; not a single answer was apparent.

It was a country music concert, of which I had never been a fan, but I was glued to the TV, bemused and bewitched by other things. He wore the obligatory tight jeans, cowboy hat and loud shirt, but I barely registered any of that. I watched his body-language, his stance in silhouette, his gestures and the way he walked, and I knew him. I listened to the words he sang, and I knew them. The song I'd heard in the shopping mall, just before that dreadful vision, was his song. It had been his voice that had triggered the scene of bloody slaughter. The song was called *The Dance*.

I felt full of wonder. I didn't have a clue what was going on, only that somehow, some way, my depression was gone. For some reason that was so inaccessible to me that it might as well have been on the other side of the Universe, seeing this man had taken away the cause of my depression. Whatever the reason for my dark despair had been, it was gone, and even more incredibly, it was gone for good, dissolved into ecstasy. It was a miracle.

By the time Tony came home from work, I'd had a couple of hours to try and figure it out, but I was still none the wiser. Tony was amazed when he saw the state I was in. I was too hyperactive to sit down.

"I don't understand..." he said.

"Neither do I. Garth Brooks, *the* answer! Now if only I knew what the question was!"

"Never mind, so long as you're better...you don't even like country music do you?"

"No, it was something else... I don't know. I can't even put it into words." I grinned at him like an idiot. Then I shrugged. I really couldn't come up with an explanation.

"What d'you know about him?"

"Not a lot...I think his songs might tell me more, especially one called *The Dance*." I looked anxiously at Tony. I really couldn't bear to have him hurt by this. "I never felt anything like this...but you know I haven't become a raving fan or anything. It's not like that at all. It's not like anything I've ever experienced."

Tony replied immediately, reassuring me. "No, it's alright. I can tell it's not like that."

The next morning I was awake, bright eyed and bushy tailed, before Tony had even stirred. I stretched languorously. Tony opened his eyes and looked at me with a slightly quizzical expression. We'd made love the night before. Not extraordinary maybe, except that *we* hadn't been that intimate for months. It's hard to switch off and relax into sex when you feel as if you have the Sword of Damocles hovering over your head the whole time.

"How do you feel this morning?" he asked.

"Great!"

"Well, there were no nightmares that I know of."

"No, I slept soundly all night."

"Really? And you still feel good?"

"I feel better than good...I feel fantastic!" I exclaimed.

"It's hard to believe...I mean, why?"

"I know...but let's not worry about why. Let's just enjoy it."

Tony leaned over and kissed me.

"And how good do you feel?" I asked mischievously. I moved my hands under the covers. I giggled. "You feel pretty good to me..."

Tony grinned and took me in his arms...

Three months later, and friends almost didn't recognise me when they saw me in the street. I'd lost a lot of weight, bringing me back to the size I'd been on our wedding day. I'd had my hair stylishly cut and streaked with blond. I'd got back into using make-up, and it helped a lot that I'd lost the bags under my eyes along with the sleepless, nightmare-ridden nights. I suddenly had a new interest in clothes, and wanted to look good.

The pain in my abdomen was still there, but subdued and somehow changed, softer; I didn't feel the need to worry about it any more, and I had no idea why. Just another question I had no answer to, just a quiet faith that it would be OK. But the biggest difference of all was that life had become imbued with an underlying excitement. I felt like something wonderful was about to happen all the time. Instead of hovering on the brink of disaster, I felt like I was standing on the edge of wonder, and anything was possible.

Whereas before every chore had seemed mundane and pointless; now I whistled and sang my way through the day. I mucked out the horses and washed up and made the beds as if there were joy in just being alive. For years Tony had been struggling in over-responsible jobs, working for bully-boy bosses. His work environment was one I'm sure many men are familiar with, where staff were laid off and never replaced, and where the extent of the jobs you were expected to do were quadrupled on a regular basis. He'd been doing this for two reasons. First, he did it for me and our son, so that we could maintain our lifestyle in the Norfolk farmhouse with its eight acres, and second, out of a misplaced sense of pride and peer pressure.

A lot of our friends were in a similar boat, and they'd fallen into the trap of believing that if they didn't have a new kitchen, carpet, and a new three-piece suite every two years, then they were a failure. I'd almost fallen into the same trap myself, but I got to thinking, Why did we do it? It seemed to me after musing on it that the reason we did all that was to impress each other. Did that work? No. It just made more pressure for everyone to keep up with each other. It created jealously and dissatisfaction. And at the end of the day, would it really matter? Was Tony wasting his health for nothing? I spent a lot of time thinking deeply.

I decided I needed to give our situation a lot of consideration. This was another change that had come over me, I felt empowered, whereas before I'd thought that life was out of my control, like being swept downstream on a leaky raft, now, suddenly I knew I could change our course. Things were going to change some day soon, for both of us.

I found out that in the US Garth Brooks was a huge star. Of course I got some of his CDs. I was intensely curious about this 'stranger' who had changed everything for us. The CDs weren't too easy to find as country music wasn't very popular with English music-lovers. I'd also tried to find information on him, to see if I could shed any light on the light he'd shed on me. But that was even harder to find. So, I contented myself with the effect, rather than searching fruitlessly for the cause.

We often played one of Garth's CDs in the evening. It seemed almost like a good luck charm; something to guard me from a resurgence of depression. The song that really struck a cord with me was *The Dance*, and we played it while we sipped a nightcap. As I listened to the words . . . *I could have missed the pain, but I'd have had to miss the dance...* I paid more attention. *Looking back, on the dance we shared...our lives are better left to chance, I could have missed the pain, but I'd have had to miss the dance.*

Something made me glance down at my hand, where it rested on the arm of the sofa. Superimposed over my own, was another hand. It was ghostly, and semi-transparent. I stared at it, transfixed. If someone had told me that this was going to happen, I would have thought it would make me afraid – a phantom, disembodied hand over-laying mine! It didn't. All I felt was warmth and comfort. I felt secure. I felt a rekindling of a time when that hand on mine had stayed all my fears, but I had no idea of how that could ever have been the case. I looked at the CD cover beside me. It was very clear. The hand I was seeing was Garth Brooks' hand, or one very much like it. His hands were quite distinctive, large and strong. His fingers had slightly 'baggy' skin over the joints, with shortish thumbs. His finger joints were very flexible, almost able to bend at 90 °. Some of these things were obvious from the photo, others I just 'knew'. Strangely, the spectral hand wore a plain gold wedding ring; unlike Garth's own one that was visible on the CD cover. I smiled, not afraid but totally content. The hand faded.

Then I started to feel more uneasy - something new was about to happen. I remembered what that song had triggered in the past. Tony and I had shared three months of blissful happiness, with no awful visions or nightmares, which I was sure was about to be shattered. *Oh my God,* I thought, *please, no…*

Tony must have noticed my preoccupation, and he asked me if I was all right. I really didn't want him to worry, so I told him I was fine. We switched off the CD player and went up to bed. I fell asleep quickly, almost as if something was calling me into the realm of dreams.

I'm looking at a castle. I know the date – it's 29 August, 1640. A

*man stands alone; a shield in his hands, no weapons. He has
brilliant blue eyes that are wide with fear. It's Garth Brooks, and yet
it isn't. Even in my dream state I am able to register that fact. The
man is dressed, not in modern country and western gear, but in
peasant's garb of the 1600s. He is thinner than Garth Brooks,
harder, and more dangerous-looking in the face, younger, and has
long black hair, dragged back into a scruffy ponytail.*

*Dozens of armed soldiers in kilts are running from the cover of a
stand of trees. I presume, given the year, that they must be Scottish.
Their faces are daubed with war-paint. They scream battle cries;
crazed with bloodlust. Behind the young man with the shield I can
see another forty or so peasants. The soldiers outnumber the others
many times over. A lot of the peasants are wounded, and they don't
have many weapons. The man with the indigo eyes drops the shield
as if his hands have petrified. He looks around and behind him. The
wounded peasant-soldiers have run to the castle and are trying to
find a sanctuary there. The first ones to reach the gates are crying
and screaming to be let in. No one will open it for them.*

*The whole thing is totally terrifying. Even though I don't feel in
personal danger, I'm deathly afraid for the man with the shield. I
want him to run, desperately, but there's nowhere for him to run to.
I can hear a rapid thud, thud, thud, my heartbeat, or his, I don't
know.*

*The blue-eyed man looks back at the rapidly advancing soldiers.
He brings both hands to his face, as if to hide the scene. His hands
slowly slide down until they cover just his mouth. His eyes though
wide with shock and fear are stunningly blue. They seem to bore into
mine. Those eyes...his eyes... I mouth his name. . . Ryan.*

His palms are together as if in prayer. He glances back over his shoulder to the men who are crying out for help. He has no choice. He reaches down and picks up the shield once more. He stands his ground as the attackers advance. The first soldier to reach Ryan swings viciously at him. The sword slices into his left arm, so that he is unable to grip the shield. He goes down under the attack. The first soldier pauses as a man running up behind him, yells, "He's mine!"

The second soldier thrusts his sword through Ryan's belly, just above the waist on his left side. As he rolls on the ground, the blade emerges from his back and his blood sprays crimson onto the green grass. So much blood. His killer reaches down and snatches the wedding ring from Ryan's hand. He shouts, "This was my Father's!" Then he runs on, triumphant, leaving his sword embedded in his victim. Ryan clutches the hilt of the sword in his right hand. He groans as the pain shakes him.

I am staring right into Ryan's face, and in his dying moments he reaches out towards me with his weak left hand. He stretches out desperately, his blood soaked fingers striving to touch me. I put my hand out too, but I can't seem to touch him and our hands pass through each other. As Ryan continues to reach out to me, he utters one final word, "Madeleine."

This time Tony had to wake me up. I was sobbing. Tony looked as scared as I felt.

The blood still filled my vision and I saw him through a veil of red. Gradually my eyes cleared. "Oh God, oh God..." I gasped.

"What? What happened?"

I answered as soon as I could, "It was horrible, they...oh...they killed him, with a sword. He's dead...Ryan's dead...He was reaching out to me...like he could see me...and I *wasn't* there for him." I started to cry, great heaving sobs that stopped me from breathing.

"All right, it's all right," he held me close until I had recovered. When I had first opened my eyes, the room had been swimming and I didn't know where or even when I was, but now I was back, safe and sound, in our bedroom.

"It was cold-blooded murder Tone. He only had a shield and this man in a kilt, just ran him through." I paused and then re-started carefully, "I don't understand how, but he was Garth Brooks too – Ryan was Garth."

"What on earth do you mean, how could…?"

"I don't know how, but I'd know those eyes anywhere."

"Why would you be dreaming about Garth Brooks being killed…?"

"I don't know, but he wasn't just Garth, he was Ryan."

"This is crazy…"

"I know…I'm sorry…" And I really was - all this dreaming about another man must have been awful for Tony. I stifled my tears.

The scene in the nightmare was the same one I had hallucinated in the shopping mall. Was I going totally insane?

I couldn't believe the nightmares were back. I had to know who Ryan was, and also where Garth Brooks figured in the equation before it drove me totally mad. I was thankful that at least the depression itself hadn't come back, at least that was gone for good. Still there were obviously some answers I had to find. *Something* wasn't going to let me go till I'd done whatever I was supposed to do. I felt that the clues to finding the answers I sought were hidden in the new nightmare. I had to find a way of unpicking the puzzle.

It's incredible how once we open, we are led. The very next day I had a horse chiropractor treating my Welsh Cob's back. To my intrigue, she used a crystal pendulum to pinpoint the source of the horse's pain. She talked about energy and healing in a way I had never heard before, and I suddenly started telling her everything that had happened to me, never even considering that she might think me mad. She listened carefully and when I told her that I couldn't understand how I *knew* someone, absolutely knew him, but had never met him, she answered me quite simply, "Not in this life maybe."

She meant in a past life. I was totally stunned. Could that really be the answer? Could I be seeing a past life? Could I have known the mysterious Ryan in another lifetime? Had Ryan been reborn as Garth Brooks? Was I who Madeleine had become? It leapt into my heart, yelling, *yes*! I intuitively knew it was true. The *rightness* of it just sat honest and pure in my soul.

OK, so it was right, but what could I do about it? How did you find out if you'd had a past life? I wanted to find out everything about Ryan and Madeleine. I wanted to understand what they had been through in that lifetime, and whether it was going to have any impact on my current life. I had so many questions that needed answering. So, I started asking people about it, particularly researching a therapy called past life regression. This was when you went to a hypnotist and they put you into a trance. This enabled them to access your subconscious, and those memories that were buried deep there, going as far back as…well I didn't know how far back they could go, but I hoped that 350 odd years wasn't too far. They could then ask you questions about the lifetime you went back to in your mind. They could find out what happened, who you'd been, who you'd known, how you had died and why, everything. It sounded scary.

Nevertheless, by the time I talked to Tony about it, I'd decided to go for past life regression under hypnosis, and as always he was understanding and supportive. He knew, as I did, that I really *had* to know. I had a horrible feeling that I had done something harmful to Ryan in that lifetime, and if I had, I wanted to be able to do something about it. What that something might be, God alone knew.

The first session sent me down a road of discovery I could never have imagined. I didn't, couldn't, think of any possible consequences to it, I just had to find out the truth. That first session left me devastated, as it took me straight to the moment that Madeleine lost Ryan forever, but it also gave me a quest to follow, a reason for being. It also told me why thinking about that life filled me with guilt, and showed me a way to heal it. It took many, many sessions, with many different therapists. It took much research on the internet, a lot of hindsight, dream interpretation, and the testimony of other people who had brief or longer memories of the same life, to uncover the whole story of Ryan and Madeleine. Some gaps were even filled in by people capable of tuning into events on a quantum level, able to step across the time lines and see the past, in the same way that clairvoyants can see the future.

I found the people who had been Ryan's mother and sisters from that life, who were able to prove conclusively to me that they were genuine. I found Ryan's half-brother Gerald, his friend Jared, Nancy the cook, and others. They are now like my soul family, and they all played their part in my future. It was many years before I realized that we do often come together with what is called our 'Soul Clan', from other lifetimes, in order to finish unfinished business from the past. With the help of these people, I was able to unravel the whole of Ryan's life, and the three years he spent with Madeleine.

It is such a beautiful, but tragic story that I'm no longer surprised by the intensity of my emotions about it, and it easily explains my depression in my current life. Madeleine lost Ryan, and for centuries her soul grieved for that loss, partly because she never really knew what had happened to him. Her unbearable grief was so deep that her soul carried it through subconsciously into *my* lifetime when she was reincarnated as me, and caused my terrible depression. That depression was disintegrated when I recognized Ryan subconsciously, because clearly he had been restored to life as Garth Brooks.

Some small gaps have had to be filled in, mostly the actual conversations, but they have been extrapolated by people who were there at the time, so I believe them to be largely correct. All the events have been independently verified. So, this is the story of Ryan and Madeleine Fitzgerald who lived, loved, and lost, in the 1600s.

CHAPTER THREE

R yan Fitzgerald was born on 16 June 1621 as James Ryan, in the county of Wexford, in Southern Ireland, but he was really the illegitimate son of Thomas Fitzgerald, the Earl of Kildare. Caitlin Ryan, James' mother, had fallen in love with the Earl and been seduced into his bed by that love. The Earl had died before James and his twin sister, Beth, were born, and for their sake Caitlin tried to keep the secret of their ancestry from her husband, John Ryan. But he found out, gossip flowing through the countryside as easily as water flowed though the rivers. John Ryan left his wife and children when James was about six years old...

On that fateful day, James, Beth, and an older sister, Patricia, all gathered around Caitlin, clinging fast to her skirt. Caitlin, petite and pretty, had dark curly hair and nut-brown eyes. She was arguing with a burly red-headed man, her husband, John Ryan. He looked very angry.

"You can't do it John - you can't take it out on the children!" Caitlin protested, desperate.

"Don't *talk* to me Caitlin! You made a fool of me! Know that I know the truth, let *Fitzgerald* take care of his own brats!"

Caitlin pleaded with him, "He's dead; you know he's dead..."

"Then let his family take care of them!"

"You know they won't. What about *your* daughter? What about Patricia? She's yours, I swear..."

"I have your word on that do I? Your word is worth *nothing*! She could be anyone's child!"

"You know that isn't true...I'm sorry..."

"Then *be* sorry - I'll not!" John Ryan grabbed his bags from the floor and stormed out.

Caitlin was left alone to care for her children, in an Ireland trapped in a time of depression, desperately trying to feed four. It was impossible. She was reduced to scrubbing floors, digging potatoes, and being used by any man who thought he had the right. She sickened; she was weak from over-work and malnutrition, and the three children often had to help her home from whatever work she had found.

Before he died, the Earl, Thomas Fitzgerald, praying for a son, had named the coming child as his rightful heir, instead of his legitimate son, Gerald. This, though done for love of Caitlin, and to help her, had actually made things worse. Threatened by it, the legitimate son, Gerald Fitzgerald, wanted nothing to do with his half-brother; for fear that he would take the right to the title, which he had claimed for himself. So when Caitlin went to plead with Gerald for help for his half-brother and half-sister, she was turned roughly away.

"Please," she'd begged of him, "Will you not help your brother and sister? Your father loved me…"

Gerald answered her scornfully, "He loved many women, and these children could be sired by someone else. Understand woman, I won't bring shame on my father's name, and I won't share my title!"

"All I understand is that my babies, your kin, are starving, while you live here in…"

"Your bastard son will have none of my inheritance. I'd rather kill him! Now get out!"

That very evening Caitlin took to her bed, and she never got out of it again. She lay there, too weak to raise her head. The three children were gathered about her. The girls were crying. James' face was white, but he didn't cry. His lips quivered, but he didn't cry. He was twelve years old. His eyes were stark, wide open, unblinking.

Caitlin spoke, her voice little more than a whisper. "Girls, my dear sweet darling girls, I want you to go outside and wait there until your brother calls you…" The girls kissed their Mother and did as she said, but unwillingly. James stood by his Mother, bending down to hear her words as her voice grew faint.

"James, I can't bear to leave you, but I have no choice."

She coughed, and a trickle of blood came from her mouth. James wiped her lips with a cloth, his strained eyes not leaving her face for a second.

"I don't know…God, I don't know how you'll cope." Her voice broke. "But you have to try…I'll be there. I'll always watch over you, wherever you are, whatever happens, I'll be there." A single tear spilled out and tracked down her cheek. "Oh my son, my beautiful son…"

"Mama…," James whispered, but she was gone. James' eyes were the bluest blue with unshed tears, and still he wouldn't cry. He kissed his mother's cheek and smoothed her hair. "I'll take care of everything Mama," he said. And he tried.

James worked as hard as he could to bring home food for his sisters. He stood doubled over for hours in the potato fields in the freezing wind, and fetched and carried for the bully boy sons of the local land-owners. Despite his best efforts Patricia grew ill and died from smallpox, and he buried her next to her mother. Beth grew steadily weaker from malnutrition. One day near the end, she was too weak to even eat the cooked half-potato he brought home for her, stolen by him at the risk of a beating if he'd been caught. That day he went to the Fitzgerald Castle himself and tried to plead with his half-brother. James was fourteen by this time and hard work had made him strong, despite not having enough to eat. He carried Beth with him to castle, hoping that the sight of her might melt a heart or two.

He argued with the gatekeeper at the castle gate. He held his sister in his arms, and she was so light that it scared him. She was pale too, and didn't seem to know where she was.

James asked the gateman, "At least ask him to take my sister, *his* sister, she's dying…"

The gatekeeper was sympathetic to the children's plight, but his hands were tied, "Sorry lad. Be on your way, afore you get into more trouble. . ."

James turned away, but then turned back, hope in his eyes, as the gatekeeper spoke again, "I'm sorry lad - really sorry…the old Master did you no favours when he named you heir…they think you might lay claim…Gerald would sooner kill you than help you."

James realised that there was no help, anywhere. He shouted at the blind Castle walls, "Then you can tell our '*brother*' that I will see his name disgraced! From this day I will no longer be 'James Ryan', but 'Ryan Fitzgerald', for the whole world to know that I am the bastard son of a Fitzgerald!"

"Be careful lad, talk like that could be dangerous…" the gatekeeper warned.

"You think I care?" James answered, as he carried Beth away. As he walked defiantly away, James decided that he would take his mother's surname, Ryan, as his first name, and the Fitzgerald surname, as his own. From that day and for the rest of his life, James

Ryan would be Ryan Fitzgerald.

Hours later he was sitting atop a lofty stone wall. It was the old wall of Ballyhack Castle, and it looked out over Waterford Estuary. His knees were bent in front of him, and he clasped his arms around them, hunkered down, staring out to sea through the curving arms of the bay. White caps flickered across the surface of the water, its perpetual variation soothing him. He could feel the cool fingers of the breeze tousling his hair, and he could taste salt on his lips. There was a mist far out to sea, and as it parted to let in the sun, it looked like a golden door opening. As the hazy shape of a ship formed on the horizon, its white sails glowing in the shaft of sunlight, the beginnings of a plan for survival began to form in his mind.

Ireland was his home, always had been, always would be in his heart, but he needed to leave home; there was danger there. His defiance meant that Gerald would want him dead. The sea would take him to freedom and safety from his half-brother. He had one more challenge to face, burying his sister as soon as she died, which he knew would be in a matter of hours. Then he'd follow where his instinct led him. His plan of traveling on a ship filled him in part with terror, but he hoped that fear's distraction would soften the blow of losing his twin sister. Besides he had no choice. Face fear or face death, not much of a choice really.

He'd been terrified of drowning ever since two wealthy land-owners' lads had repeatedly ducked him in a farm pond. The sight of deep water filled him with dread as he recalled the horror of his stomach filling with rancid water, and breathing it in when the air in his lungs had run out. Thinking of distractions; he sighed, and got up. He had to go back. When he'd left home an hour since, it had been because he didn't think he could face it, not again, God, not again… not little Beth. He still didn't think he could face it, but there was no choice. He'd left her alone for too long already.

When he got back to the shabby hovel he called home, Beth was asleep on the rug in front of the fire, where he'd left her. Her tiny wasted body was peaceful, and she breathed evenly. He banked up the fire by throwing on the last of the broken table legs, and still she didn't stir. He sat down in the old wooden chair, his fingers tracing the grains of the wood of the arms, made smoother by his mother's touch over the years. He couldn't bear to burn that chair, the last trace of his mother. Beth became restless, moaning in her sleep. Ryan got up and lifted her. He realized he was crying. He wanted to scream out, *No! I can't lose her too!* He knew it was no use, so his tears remained silent. He sat back down, cradling her on his lap. He began to gently rub the top of her head, his fingers tangling and untangling her dark hair. It had always calmed her, and it did so again. She settled.

By 2am Ryan was dozing, Beth still curled in his lap. He awoke as instinct warned him that her breathing had become ragged and shallow. With no more sign, it just stopped. He gasped and hugged her to him convulsively, and she breathed fitfully again. He remained tense, clutching her to him, willing each breath, his tears again filling his eyes and overflowing, falling onto her upturned face. He held her tightly, she was all he had. As her breathing slowed further, he knew there was no more he could do to keep her. She belonged with her mother…but if he let her go, then he would be alone! The feeling terrified him. He closed his eyes, unable to watch Beth as she struggled to stay alive for him.

He pictured himself standing on the prow of a ship; huge waves lifting and dropping the deck beneath his feet. The fear he felt of the bottomless sea beneath him took him away from Beth's final struggle. Then he felt an angel soft touch on his cheek, and he opened his eyes to harsh reality again. Her thin hand stroked his cheek and his mouth. She was too weak to speak, but she smiled at him. Then her breath halted, and she was gone. Sobs burst from him. Now he was all alone, and he knew he had failed them all.

He sat there as his tears dried, and she grew cold, and he felt a coldness growing in him. Never again would he allow himself to feel love for anyone else. It was too hard. Brick by brick he built a wall around his heart. No-one would ever breach it again, no-one. No-one would ever rely on him again, he couldn't take it.

Dawn found him at the grave where his mother and elder sister had already been buried. As he was sifting the last handful of dirt onto Beth's grave, he saw a group of horsemen riding over the hill. They yelled when they saw him. Gerald had wasted no time! With a last sad look at the three small, unmarked mounds of earth, Ryan threw down the spade and ran. He felt like a hunted stag, and terror made it hard to run fast because it had taken his breath.

But after a while, after twisting and turning through the hedgerows, banks, and ditches, which he knew like the back of his hand, he lost them, and he slowed to a purposeful walk. He reached the docks by mid-afternoon, and managed to get passage to England on a ship that was lacking crew, enough to take on an untrained man. He was on board and the ship had cast off and was gently slipping away from the harbour wall, when he saw the gateman from the Castle running alongside the quay. Then several horsemen appeared on the causeway and galloped after the gateman. The gateman looked scared but he still ran alongside the ship as the gap between it and the harbour wall grew.

As he drew level, the gateman shouted up to Ryan, "Lad! Take this! It was your father's. It's precious little, but it proves your right, I reckon!" He tossed something to Ryan. It was a gold ring, and it glittered as it spun in the sunlight. Ryan snatched the ring from the air just in time as the ship moved out of reach of the shore, and he could do nothing but look back in horror as the mounted men fell upon the gateman, and he vanished beneath hooves and hands.

When the shore and the fight had faded into the horizon, Ryan opened his fist and looked at the ring. It was plain gold, but when he held it up to the light he could read an inscription etched on it, 'Crom abu.' He shook his head as he read it, because its meaning, of support for home and family seemed denied to him. The ring was too big for all except his middle finger. He put it on his right hand, but then as an afterthought, took it off again. It would be too tempting for a thief in plain sight. He went below and found a piece of fine rope and threaded it through the ring. Then he placed the rope around his neck, knotted it, and pushed the ring inside his shirt, where it laid on his chest.

Ryan grew afraid as the ship sailed out into deep water. Beneath the deck he could feel an abyss as deep and dark as the night sky. He felt that if he were to fall overboard, he wouldn't float on the arms of the salty sea water, but would rather plummet to his death at the bottom of a fathomless void. Gradually as the voyage went on and he was subject to gruelling work and the camaraderie of his shipmates, his panic attacks grew less. There was no escape from the ship after all, and this vessel was at least taking him away from mortal danger.

CHAPTER FOUR

Meanwhile, in Hambledon, in the county of Hampshire in England, Madeleine was growing up. Her real mother, Rebecca, had died when her only child was six years old. Despite Madeleine's young age, her father, Edwin, had allowed her to take up the role of 'the lady of the house', in order to ease her grief. Father and daughter had slowly been making a new life without Rebecca, but when Madeleine was ten years old, a woman called Margaret Beresford had come into their lives. Edwin quickly decided to marry Margaret, without any warning to Madeleine, and Margaret had been introduced to the child for the first time as her father's new wife, and her new mother, all at the same time.

Madeleine had seen through her young and knowing eyes that Margaret didn't love Edwin. She was much younger than her husband, and had married him, Madeleine was sure, just to improve her station in life. This seemed to be the truth because Margaret soon insisted that they move to a bigger house. She didn't seem to know or care that by doing so she was tearing the little girl from her last connections with Rebecca, her real Mother.

The house was built on parkland, hunting land. It had originally been the Park-keeper's home, but the late 16th century had seen it extended. This was in part to provide a secret room between old and new, so that Catholic priests outlawed by the monarchy could hide there, safe from prying eyes if they were interrupted while holding a mass for the occupants. The extension was a three-storey tower, which also provided a newer and bigger kitchen and dining room than had been there before, and servants' quarters on the top storey.

The priest's hole was neatly slotted in between the old and new wings. The parkland still surrounded the house, with sweeping grassland dotted with majestic trees, perfect land for deer. There was also a dairy, sometimes used for cider-making, extensive stables and two tithe barns.

The next few years brought constant animosity between the new wife and the young daughter. By the time Madeleine was thirteen years old, and Ryan was losing his own mother in Ireland, there was all-out war between the two women. Their constant bickering made Edwin tired. He was a politician and was away in London a lot of the time. When he was home he would have liked peace and quiet, but rarely got it.

Between the woman who was his wife, and his soon-to-be-a-woman daughter, Edwin was pulled to and fro like a rag between two dogs. After a while it became obvious that Margaret was the stronger willed, and Madeleine would often give up the fight. This suited Edwin, because his young and feisty wife was unable to let go of any argument until she won. Edwin got used to standing on the side of Margaret, and Madeleine got used to losing. Madeleine spent as little time in the house as she could, running off to the fields and woods whenever she got the chance. After a while she couldn't be bothered to be defiant. She felt free because she cared for no-one and felt no-one cared for her. The only saving grace in her life was Nancy, the cook. This motherly woman treated Madeleine like a daughter and kept her sane in a fragmented household.

Ryan's ship came ashore at Southampton. He headed off, full of optimism for his new life. He intended to head towards the city of London, but he wasn't used to finding his way, and his chosen path actually took him north-west. He didn't know what his future might hold, but at least he was responsible now for just one person, himself, and he was determined that it would remain that way.

His very first encounter with Englishmen after landing did not endear them to him. His initial optimism had been tempered by the twenty miles he had covered without finding any welcoming place to stay. He was wearily plodding down a narrow country lane, not knowing where he might find food or shelter, and with a growing terror of being totally alone in the world, with no-one to care whether he lived or died. Being independent had its drawbacks after all. He missed the camaraderie of life on board ship, even though the work had been so hard and even though he had been very relieved to step onto dry land again.

The lane he found himself on was dark and closed in. He could see no beauty in his surroundings. Tall trees and thick hedges blocked the sun's rays and the prevailing gloom seemed ominous. It was too quiet after the bustle on board ship. His footfalls made almost no sounds at all, as if the atmosphere was just swallowing them up. He felt as if he was walking down a tunnel that would grow ever darker around him, until eventually he merely winked out of existence.

Suddenly, from behind the tall hedge that flanked the lane, the real world interrupted his solitude with a frightful commotion. The excited baying of hounds poured towards him, and this was punctuated by the high-pitched, petrified bleating of an animal in mortal fear. There was a small gap at the bottom of the hedge, and without any thought as to what he might find on the other side, Ryan scrambled through it.

His actions from then on were purely instinctive, with no reasoning, for he found a creature there that was more powerless than he felt. Its helplessness actually made him feel more powerful. In the corner of the meadow, where a tall hedge that bounded the field made an open-ended triangle with the gated entrance into another field, there stood a trapped female red deer and her newborn fawn. The fawn was all wide and terrified eyes, and long, unsteady legs. The doe could normally have jumped the gate with ease but her fawn could not, so she stayed with it. She faced a small pack of hunting hounds as she tried futilely to protect her infant. This pathetic yet heroic display of maternal courage touched Ryan's heart deeply and he felt not fear of the pack, but fury. The doe was already bleeding from several dog bites, and she was groaning pitifully.

Ryan ran among the hounds and got between them and their prey. He tore a thick branch from the hedgerow, put his back to the flagging deer, and began to swing his weapon at the circling pack. They backed off, confused by an attack from a human. Ryan took advantage of this, and yelled at them. The deer on the other hand seemed less afraid of him than of the dogs and stood behind him, panting. The pack retreated further, and Ryan used this respite to dive at the gate, dragging and lifting it through the long grass as it protested on its rusty hinges, until the gap was enough. The deer, sensing escape, brushed past Ryan, bounded through the gap and sped across the next field, closely followed by her fawn. The hounds surged forward but Ryan continued to hold them off, swinging the branch like a sword, stopping them from taking up pursuit again.

There came the sound of horsemen. There were ten of them, and they pounded across the field, their shouts reaching him long before they did. They could see their quarry escaping and this wild figure slashing at their hounds with a branch. They were obviously very angry at the disruption to their day's sport, and they drove their horses into the mêlée, scattering the hounds. Ryan was buffeted by them until with a furious shout one rider brought his fist down heavily on Ryan's shoulder, knocking him to the ground. Hooves flashed at him, one catching him a sharp blow to his leg, and Ryan would bear the imprint of its shoe on his thigh for many weeks. But as he lay bruised and battered in the grass, the scent of the crushed vegetation filling his nostrils, he looked over his shoulder, and had the great satisfaction of seeing the deer and her fawn reach the far side of the field, disappearing into the woodland there, well ahead of her pursuers.

Ryan picked himself up, and for his own safety ran back to the hedge and scrambled through it into the lane. He set off down it as fast as he could. Although his leg hurt, his spirits soared and there was a bounce in his step. He glanced back over his shoulder many times to make sure that he hadn't become the prey of the hunt, having deprived them of their original victim. The plight of the poor deer and her baby had made him feel stronger. There were others worse off than him after all. The trees and hedges now formed a conspiring barrier, shielding him from the eyes of the hunters, and the inky lane was his friend, and he welcomed the near silence of his footsteps. As he trotted onwards the sun glinted in places through the hedgerow, highlighting the pretty wildflowers that grew at the edge of the lane, turning the damp tunnel into a safe and secret garden.

After a worrying few weeks, during which time Ryan had to sleep outdoors and gather what food he could from the hedgerows and fields, he found work on a farm near the village of Charlton Marshall. He was reasonably happy there, although his only bed was in the barn, and there was never enough food. He was always hungry, but he could not really remember ever feeling any other way.

He had to leave there eventually because Marian, the farmer's sixteen-year-old daughter, was becoming too fond of him, and his wariness of love and attachment meant that he had to move on. This was life for him in any case, never seeing too many dawns in the same place, ever fearful of leaving too much of his scent anywhere, in case his brother chose to follow him across the Irish Sea.

After leaving the farm, he passed by an Abbey Church, in the village of Middleton, and thought it the most beautiful building he had ever seen. It sat like a jewel in a green bowl, perfect in design and symmetry, almost as if it had grown there naturally.

Two weeks later, hungry and exhausted, he called at a small farm and got employment and lodgings with the farmer's widow. He was pleasantly surprised, because at first sight the farm and cottage didn't look prosperous enough to employ anyone. But Glenda Miles, the owner of the farm, seemed in no doubt that she wanted him to stay. She took him by the hand and drew him into the cosy cottage, seating him on the settle in front of the fire. She then prepared him the best meal he had seen for years. He fell asleep as soon as he had finished eating, and did not wake up until the next morning.

Glenda was a Welshwoman by birth, a buxom lady with laughing brown eyes and long, curly flaxen hair. She took one look at the handsome young man who appeared suddenly on her doorstep, like a gift from God, and decided that she should be the one to teach him the arts of love. Her husband had been gone two years, and had been a lot older than her. She was about to remarry, to a wealthy old man, and she welcomed Ryan's presence and youth as a chance to dance with the wind, one last time.

Ryan slept each night on the settle whilst Glenda slept in the only bedroom upstairs in the cottage. On the Friday night, Glenda told him with a twinkle in her eye that he did now know how to interpret, that after she had gone to bed, he could bathe in front of the fire in the tin bath.

Glenda crouched in the curving stairwell behind the door while Ryan filled the bath. It seemed to take forever for him to heat enough water over the fire. The room was clouded with steam from multiple kettles of boiling water by the time there was enough in the bath to use. Wisps of steam filtered through the gap at the door, making Glenda's skin damp and pink, as she waited. She heard Ryan undress and climb into the bath, and the sound of water slopping over the sides onto the flagstone floor. She waited a few more minutes for him to clean himself, anticipation heightening her excitement.

When she crept into the room behind him, he was still luxuriously lathering himself, and did not realize straight away that she was there. She stood there quietly for a few moments watching him. Finally he sensed her presence and peered over his shoulder. She smiled at him. She was totally naked. Ryan's eyes grew wide as she walked round into his full sight. The expression of sheer wonderment in his eyes confirmed for her that he had never slept with a woman before.

Ryan just stared. Glenda walked up to the bath, smiling again at his stunned look. He swallowed nervously, as Glenda reached into the soapy water and started to run her hands over him. His body was firm and pleasingly shaped. The soapy water made her touch glide like silk over his skin. Then she reached down into the water and started to stroke him rhythmically. It was too much for him, as she had expected it would be, and with a loud moan, Ryan climaxed.

"I am sorry," he gasped, "I've never…"

"Good," she purred. "It will be easier now. Come with me." This was all working out beautifully for her. She took his hand, and drew him out of the bath, and led him, still soaking wet, upstairs to her bedroom. There she told him to lie on her bed, climbed up beside him, and drew him over on top of her.

Later she taught him in how to explore her body's most intimate secrets. During that night, and every night for the following month, he became assured and confident, learning to control his own body, and learning exactly where and when to touch her to give her most pleasure. She was well pleased with her student, and when he told her that he wouldn't be able to stay forever, she reassured him that nothing could be further from her mind. She told him that she was to be wed for the third time and that, though it saddened her, Ryan would have to leave soon in any case. Her new husband's family would soon arrive to help her to make the move to London, where he lived. So Ryan had to go, before his presence was discovered. He left his latest home, and once more began to journey towards London, this time heading in more or less the right direction, working wherever he could and eating whenever he could.

Ryan eventually came to the small town of Hambledon in Hampshire. It was a seemingly nice place, but he had no idea at the time that he would spend almost the rest of his life there. He never dreamed that he would meet someone there that he would want to stay with forever. He stopped at the Green Man Inn, and thanks to a recent good spell of work he was able to afford the luxury of a jug of ale and some bread and cheese. He still felt hungry afterwards, for hard toil and small meals never produced a satisfied stomach.

Eventually he left the inn, having asked about work locally, and later in the afternoon he strode along a narrow grassy track heading north east out of Hambledon. He had been told that the track would lead him to **** House, where he might find work in exchange for lodgings.

CHAPTER FIVE

Madeleine was fourteen years old. On that day she was riding her horse, fast, along an overgrown grass lane, away from the house. She was riding astride, which was a bit uncomfortable in the long dress she wore, but that was how she liked to ride. She was driving the horse along, full of anger. Margaret had started yet another argument, going on and on about Madeleine finding a 'suitable' young man and bringing his fortune into their house. Men! Madeleine hated men! They were no use for anything as far as she could tell. They did the rough work, that was true, but no better, in her opinion than the women could have done, given the chance. Her father was a poor example, being a sad and weak man, constantly manipulated by his clever wife.

Her mind not on her riding, going too fast for the terrain, Madeleine failed to notice a thick tree branch at head-height in time to avoid it, and it struck her sharply on the top of her head. With the sudden searing pain came dizziness. She fell from the horse and the force of hitting the ground winded her. She passed out. Her horse ran on a few yards, and then stopped and started to graze on the lush grass.

Moments later two youths suddenly appeared from the bushes, and the horse threw its head up, startled, and trotted off a few paces before settling again. The youths paused for a moment, assessing the situation.

The first youth spoke, "Ere, what's this then?"

The other one answered, "Looks like me birthday! Come on!"

They hurried over to where Madeleine was sprawled on the

ground. The first youth bent down and stroked her hair.

"Pretty," he commented

The other one responded gruffly, "Never mind that - we might not 'ave much time."

His partner in crime dropped to his knees beside Madeleine and started to lift her skirt, which wasn't easy due to the fullness of it, while the other one looked around nervously. Moments later he had forgotten to keep a lookout, as he was too busy staring lecherously at his friend's attempts to push up Madeleine's skirt. The first youth had to lift her bodily, in order to free the skirt from underneath her.

His companion also dropped to his knees beside her and started to fumble with her dress, with "Ere, let me…"

"Me first - get off!" he was told.

He stood up again and started to undo the top of his britches, and his intent was obvious, as he didn't take his eyes off Madeleine's bare legs.

A third young man approached. It was Ryan. He was young, tall, and although quite thin, he was well muscled from his years of physical labour. He had long black hair tied back in a ponytail. Some of his hair had come loose and it trailed over his face. Violet-blue eyes could be glimpsed through the unruly strands of dark hair. He had a full, well-shaped mouth and a wide jaw. He was wearing a white shirt, breeches and knee-length boots, with a frieze (woollen coat) over the top. His clothes were well-worn and dirty. He carried a bag over one shoulder. Paths were about to be crossed, and two young people would have their lives changed forever.

The two youths were so busy arguing over their spoils that they failed to notice the dark young man's approach. Assessing the situation quickly, he threw his bag to the ground and ran towards

Madeleine's would-be attackers. He didn't shout, but came almost silently. He cannoned into one youth from behind and sent him sprawling, thumping him hard on the back of his neck as he went down. The second youth rose to his feet with a cry. The rescuer head-butted him, and he staggered, his nose smeared red with blood. His attacker just stood and looked at him for a second or two, a ferocious glower on his face. The first youth got up, grabbed his friend's arm and motioned him to come away. The two ruffians ran off.

Ryan looked at Madeleine as she remained still, sprawled on the ground. He picked up his bag and then crouched on his haunches at a short distance from her, obviously unsure of what he should do next. He was loath to touch her; probably because his actions might be misconstrued. He rubbed his hand over his face as he considered what to do. Her skirt was still rucked-up around her thighs, but if he had tried to pull it down and she woke up while he was doing it, she could well have misinterpreted his actions.

Madeleine groaned and started to sit up. She glanced down at her bare legs and hurriedly pulled her skirt down. Pleased that she seemed all right, Ryan scuttled towards her on his hands and knees. She drew back with a gasp; clearly frightened of him. Immediately he stopped, and smiled. His voice, when he spoke, was a soft Irish lilt.

"Have no fear My Lady. I'll not harm you. I've just seen off those cowards who would have hurt you."

A moment of silence passed. Ryan smiled again. Their eyes met. His were a deep intense blue, hers a lighter grey-blue. There was a second or two of unspoken communication between souls. A slow smile formed on Madeleine's face.

Ryan held out a hand, "Can you stand?"

Madeleine winced and touched her head where the branch made contact. "I think so, with your help." She took his hand and he drew her to her feet.

"What's your name?" Madeleine asked him.

"Ryan Fitzgerald, Miss."

"I'm Madeleine de Port."

Madeleine insisted that Ryan should accompany her home. She told him that her father would be as impressed with the rescuing of his daughter, and that he would probably reward him and offer him a job and lodgings on the spot. However, she was in for a shock.

Margaret greeted Ryan's sudden arrival in her drawing room with total horror. She glared at him with venom, despite his mortified expression, and her face showed only more horror as she listened to Madeleine's explanation of who he was and how they had met. Edwin, looking every one of his sixty years and more, leaned against the mantle for support.

Margaret was restless and paced around, very agitated, while Ryan stood to one side, looking awkward.

Margaret finally stopped, poised, staring at Ryan. Her eyes slowly raked him from his head to his feet. Her lips curled in distaste at the scruffiness of the young man who stood in her territory. Ryan looked down at his own feet, obviously uncomfortable with the scrutiny. Finally she raised her eyes up again and spoke, "Just a vagabond. He looks like a gypsy."

Madeleine asked angrily, "How can you be so cold and offensive? If it weren't for him I'd have been assaulted and disgraced!"

Margaret spat back at her, "We only have your word for it that he didn't *instigate* the assault. What he might have done to you while you were dazed, heaven alone knows!"

Edwin tried to pacify them both, obviously embarrassed at having family arguments aired in front of a stranger. "Madeleine, Margaret, my dears, let's continue this discussion in private, please." He gestured to Ryan and told him to make himself scarce to the kitchen, where he would be fed. Ryan left the room quickly, relief on his face.

Madeleine went over to her father and put her arm possessively through his, smiling up at him, "Father, please don't make him leave. He was courageous, and he *did* help me, I swear. He's strong, and you need more workers on the farm."

Edwin wavered, "You know nothing about him…"

Madeleine's voice softened to a whisper, "But I *do* know him…I trust him"

Edwin looked from his wife to his daughter and back, in indecision. Margaret was scowling and Madeleine was grinning. Unusually, perhaps sensing that this time it was different, Edwin stood up to his wife in favour of his daughter. "Very well child. He may sleep in the barn, and take his fixings from the kitchen. But I'll expect hard work in exchange mind!"

Margaret was furious with this turn of events, "Edwin! Really! Is she never to learn obedience to me?"

"Enough! Please my dear. I'm weary. Let it rest, for now."

Madeleine fell in love with the young Irishman instantly, and she showed it naturally and guilelessly. Ever since he came to her on that fateful day, she had been intrigued and entranced by him. She loved the way he talked to her. She'd been totally bored on the many occasions when her Stepmother had tried to interest her in the sons of local gentry, or even worse in the indubitably, excruciatingly, dull Mr Pennington. He was fat, old, and boring, whereas Ryan...she adored his physique, which was strong and powerful, although he treated her with the utmost gentility. His eyes were the rarest true blue, his lashes were long and jet; and his mouth extravagantly full and inviting. Surely, a mouth meant for kissing. She knew nothing of kissing, but it seemed to her that this must be true.

Days after his arrival, she stood and watched him working in the garden. He was turning over the soil. She walked closer to him from behind. He wasn't aware of her and carried on working, while she watched in silence. Her admiration for him was obvious in her expression. She just stared at him silently, a smile on her lips, transfixed. Ryan was lean but strong, with a powerful frame. He turned over the soil effortlessly; it was obviously something he was well used to.

Weeks later Ryan and Madeleine walked next to each other along a wooded path, not touching.

Madeleine spoke, "I love to walk with you."

Ryan looked very uneasy; "I enjoy your company also, but if your mother..."

Madeleine almost snapped back, "She is *not* my mother!" His eyes widened slightly, and her voice softened, "Even if she was, I wouldn't care what she thought...I...oh!

She seemed to trip, and before Ryan could register that the trip was contrived, he automatically put out his hand to steady her. Madeleine turned to him and moved really close, putting her hand over his where it held her arm, looking up at him. He immediately lowered his hand and backed away a step.

"Miss..."

They stared at each other, their eyes locked.

They walked side by side. Madeleine reached out and took hold of Ryan's hand, threading her fingers through his. He looked down at their hands, but he didn't pull away. They sat side by side on a fallen log. They were talking quietly and then Madeleine rested her head companionably on Ryan's shoulder.

Things never moved quickly enough for Madeleine. For a long time Margaret had had everything she wanted it seemed, and although Madeleine hadn't been exactly unhappy, she had felt very alone. It had been time for Madeleine to have something her own way for once. Now this beautiful young man with his sapphire eyes had come into her life, and she was so happy that she expected everyone else would be happy too. How could they not be? But Ryan obviously wasn't convinced. She knew he felt the same about her, but apart from holding her hand, he never touched her. She longed for him to kiss her, but he never did. The day after her fifteenth birthday she decided that she had to find a way to let Ryan know that it was all right for him to show his feeling towards her.

At night, lying in her bed, all she could think of was him. All she wanted was him. It was up to her to take the first step. She could picture Ryan all too clearly in his bed of straw in the barn. He was so close and yet so far. She felt dizzy with longing. She had no idea of what she actually wanted from him, but she knew she had to just go to him, and so one night she did. She got out of bed, pulled a robe on over her nightgown and crept downstairs. Tiptoeing through the kitchen she went outside, gasping as her bare feet touched the cold flagstones of the yard. The small barn where Ryan slept was just across the yard, and moonlight lit her way, splashing against the barn door like a beacon. She pulled the barn door open and peeped inside.

She couldn't resist the lure of him.

Inside the barn Ryan was asleep in a bed of straw, much as she had pictured him, naked under a heavy blanket that was pulled up to his waist, leaving his chest bare. As soon as Madeleine stepped through the doorway he was aware of her. Through slits in his eyes he watched her as she stepped closer – closer. She stopped, and her eyes were fixed on the soft rise and fall of his chest. As she moved towards him again her breath was fast and fearful as if she was walking towards a sleeping tiger. She sat down softly on the straw and stared at him.

Ryan's every nerve-ending was tingling. Part with fear of what would happen if she were discovered, and part with excitement at her nearness. He knew that he could not, dare not, react to her as she obviously wanted, because to do so would surely bring him death. Maybe if she thought him sleeping, she would leave. He needed her to leave. He was desperate for her to stay.

After a while Madeleine reached out and touched his hair with a feather-like gentleness, where it lay in disarray around his head. He didn't stir. She grew bolder, and softly trailed a fingertip across the palm of his upturned hand. Still he didn't move.

"Are you truly sleeping?" she whispered. She reached up to touch his cheek and, as her fingers were about to brush his skin, Ryan could stand it no longer and his eyes flicked open. His heart and body totally ignored the warnings his mind was screaming at them. His hands ached to touch her. She sat staring at him in the moonlight, and her hair was a golden halo around her head. He could smell the scent of her. He wanted her, and he had since the first moment he saw her. He dared, just for a few minutes, to dream that she could be his.

Madeleine gasped. Ryan was staring at her, his eyes glinting with need. She looked confused and embarrassed. She started up, poised to flee, like a startled deer. Then Ryan smiled like the sun coming from behind a cloud, just like on the first day they'd met. She returned his smile, and they looked at each other silently for a few heartbeats. Then, without warning, he reached up and grasped her hands. He pulled her down to him, so that her body fell onto his, her captive hands pinned between them, as he put his arms around her.

"I've longed to love you," his voice whispered, while his mind screamed, *Don't be a fool!*

Their lips met, and her mouth melted into his. Her hands were cool against the hot skin of his chest, and cold fire coursed right through his body.

Suddenly Madeleine pulled back, but he held her firm against him. She struggled for a few seconds and then subsided, letting her body mould to his. At that moment he could have made any use of her that he wished, but in the end it was he who stopped.

My God, he thought, *what am I doing?* He pulled away from her so that she rolled in an undignified way back onto the hay. He pushed himself up into a sitting position, careful to take his rug with him. He was unable to meet her eyes.

"Forgive me," he murmured quietly.

Sitting back up she protested, "But it was my own doing. I came upon you in sleep."

"No," he said, "You don't understand. Madeleine…" He was thinking quickly, trying to find a way to undo what he had done. He continued, "I didn't realise it was you." The lie was all he could think of.

"No," she protested. The moonlight; you knew it was me!"

But before she could protest further he said, "It's impossible, I can't love you, no-one would allow it."

"It doesn't matter what anyone else thinks," she answered. "I care only for you."

His eyes met hers, searchingly; "Is that how you really feel?" He found he *could* believe it, and for a second everything seemed possible.

"It's true," she answered him. "I want nothing more at this moment than to lie with you all night."

No, it couldn't be. It could never happen. He'd been fooling himself. He would *not* love her. Anyway she had no idea what the consequences of her wishes would be. "You don't know what you're saying," he insisted, "You're unknowing. I don't want to give your parents anything to use against us."

"Ryan, it doesn't matter what my parents think. I love you. I know you love me too. Surely that's all that matters? You do love me, don't you?"

"No...no, of course not...and I have many female friends...I thought you were one of the servant girls from the manor."

"But...you *love* me!"

Things were spiralling out of Ryan's control. He felt panic-stricken. He forced himself to shut down. He'd become good at that over the years in Ireland. His expression closed down, a sullen and cold façade. He dropped a mental barrier between them and Madeleine stiffened as if she had felt it.

"I don't love. I can't love. Please..." he said, refusing to look at her, and staring fixedly at the straw on the barn floor, "...leave me alone and go back to the safety of your bedchamber. I don't desire you." He had no choice. He had to make her leave somehow, and quickly. Hurt was the only way. His heart pounded frantically at the thought of someone coming into the barn and catching them together. His mind raced at the consequences of letting himself love someone, or letting someone love him, rely on him, and relief swept through him when she scrambled to her feet. He deliberately refused to see the expression of hurt and bewilderment on her face, otherwise he might have weakened.

Madeleine fled the barn, a devastated look on her face. She slammed the door behind her, and leaned back against it, sobs bursting from her. Now the cold moonlight blinded her, embarrassed her, like a floodlit actor on a stage who has forgotten his lines. She was confused and humiliated. He'd said that he longed to love her with one breath and yet in the next he had sent her away, saying he didn't love her at all. She'd offered him all she had and he'd refused it. She felt crushed. Furiously, her mind twisted, trying to make some sense of it all, a way to live with what he had done to her. She would never have dreamed that Ryan would have been able to be so cruel to her. She ran across the yard in tears, but as the moonlight followed her, she stopped and stood in its white power, revelation flooding over her just as the light from the moon did. She spoke out loud to it, "I know he loves me! He's just afraid! And one day I'd make him admit it!"

For a time, Ryan kept his distance from Madeleine. If he'd intended to hurt her, he couldn't have cut her heart deeper. She struggled to understand what was going on in his mind. She constantly wrestled with how he could have said he wanted her, and then acted so differently. She was aware from talk among the workers that Ryan wasn't inexperienced as she was. She had no knowledge of men at all. Perhaps that had something to do with it, she thought, *maybe even his passionate kissing was a fraud meant to frighten this foolish child away. But I felt that passion; surely I couldn't have felt it so strongly if he hadn't felt it too?* No, something else was holding him back from showing his true feelings, he was afraid, and she would have to find a way to make him forget his fear.

As the months passed by, Ryan and Madeleine were never alone, because he made certain of it, always walking away if she came near, keeping in the company of others as much as he could so that she had no chance to challenge him. If he was as unhappy as her then he never showed it.

CHAPTER SIX

S everal months later things came to a head. Madeleine was standing watching Ryan gouging rocks out of some virgin soil with a pick-axe, making it ready for tilling. As usual of late he was working with another man alongside him, so that she would be afraid to speak to him, but he had reckoned without her desperation. She walked closer to him, and he ignored her. She couldn't stand it. It felt like she'd lost everything, including her best friend, and so she spoke, never caring that another man was listening to the words of her heart.

"Ryan! *Please!*"

He carried on working, but glanced sidelong at her, the sweep of his long eyelashes, and the hyacinth-blue of his wide eyes tearing at her heart. She was overwhelmed with love for him. The other worker glanced curiously at the two of them.

Ryan swallowed hard, registering the man's interest, and spoke blandly, "Beg pardon Miss - did you require some service of me?"

She asked herself, *how could he talk to me like that? As if I were the mistress of the house and he was my servant, lowly and humble.*

"I think you know what I require of you!" she paused, and then the love in her voice was obvious, "Ryan I want you to talk to me, like you used to. Before I…" She looked down, "…before I came to your bed." she could feel the heat in her face as she blushed, and the other worker's eyes widened in total shock, "I want us to be how we were. I want your friendship. *Please - Ryan!"*

Ryan took a deep breath. He glanced at the workman next to him, who was staring at him incredulously. That man's thoughts were easy to read, but Ryan blinked his away, and his answer made Madeleine's heart plummet to the ground. "I'm sorry Miss, but I have my work to do. The Mistress doesn't pay me to talk."

Her pain made her angry with him, "Oh, you're impossible! Why hide your feelings so much? You love me and it won't always be like this!" She strode off, too angry and hurt and humiliated to try any more.

Further along Madeleine met Nancy. Confidante and surrogate mother, Madeleine relied on her always, with complete trust. Nancy had become Madeleine's replacement mother after her natural mother Rebecca had died, and even more so since Margaret had arrived. She was the only person in the house who loved Ryan nearly as much as Madeleine did. He was even putting on weight now that she was in charge of feeding him. When Ryan had first come to the house she had all but adopted him at first sight.

Taking in Madeleine's facial expression she asked, "Is something amiss my dear? You look a little flushed."

"I'm angry Nancy!"

"Angry? With whom?"

"With Ryan!"

Nancy immediately bristled like a mother hen, "Why?"

"It's nothing." Madeleine paused, trying to put her thoughts into words without shocking Nancy too much. "He loves me, I'm sure he loves me, and yet he won't even talk to me now. He used to. For months he was my best friend, but now…"

"He used to? He's changed? How? I won't have him hurt you."

"I have to tell you everything. Maybe you can explain it to me. But *she* must never hear of it."

"What is it that I must never tell? I'll not betray you."

"I went to him, in the barn, in the night." Madeleine felt her flush rise again at the confession because she knew Nancy would be shocked by it.

Madeleine was right; Nancy was horrified and exclaimed, "*Miss!* What happened?"

"Nothing! Nothing happened…well a kiss. That's what vexes me so!"

"A kiss? Oh my…"

"He rejected me, denied that he loved or desired me! But it wasn't true, I'm certain. Certain! And now… now he won't even look at me."

Nancy was looking more alarmed by the second, "Miss, oh my sweet child. Thank the Lord that Ryan had the sense…"

"Sense? It was cruel!"

"You and he can't be together in that way. He'd be driven out, or worse, if he ever used you."

"How could he be accused of using me when it was I who wanted it?" Even as she said it, Madeleine knew that what Nancy said was true, but she couldn't admit it, that would be like admitting there was no hope, ever.

"Your stepmother has plans for you. She'd be incensed if she knew what's been going on." Nancy shuddered at the notion, "Oh my word, I can see her face now. Ryan will never approach you or encourage you in this, not if he values his life."

A sob broke from Madeleine. She couldn't hold it back, "And what if *I* no longer value *my* life without *him?* What then?"

Madeleine ran off, leaving Nancy to make her way onwards to where Ryan was working. Her heart was breaking. She had never imagined that loving someone could be so painful. Then she had a thought. Nancy would speak to Ryan about what she'd said, of course she would, and he confided in the cook as much as Madeleine did…so, she made her way behind the bushes at the side of the track, and kept pace with Nancy, hidden from her sight. Madeleine knew it was wrong to eavesdrop, but she had to know. Maybe Ryan would say something that would show her the truth of how he felt.

Madeleine was right; when Nancy reached Ryan, she stopped and watched him work, much as Madeleine had done. Finally, with a sigh, he stopped working and looked at Nancy.

"What is it?"

"I was just talking to Miss Madeleine."

Ryan turned away and slammed his pickaxe into the ground with unnecessary force. "Oh." He raised a hand to silence her and turned to the workman at his side, "Go back to the cows now, I can manage here." The man looked at him, irritation written clear on his face. Ryan stared back and the man dropped his gaze and walked away. Ryan waited until he was well out of earshot, before turning to Nancy again, "I've given them enough to talk about already today."

Nancy started again as if there had never been a pause. "Oh? That's all you have to say? She told me that she came to you in your bed."

Ryan took a deep breath and struck the ground again with the pickaxe. "Oh."

"Oh? Again oh? Ryan she'll be the *death* of you!"

"Do you think I don't know that? I did nothing. I left her in no doubt that it was impossible."

"Impossible to you or me perhaps, but Madeleine…"

"What else can I do?"

"You can leave. Get as far away from here as you can. Take one of the serving girls from the manor with you. There are plenty who'd be willing. That will put the Master and Mistress off the scent. "

"I can't." He drew the pickaxe back and slammed it into the ground with all his strength. Breathless, he paused, leaning on the handle. "I can't leave her… Those others are nothing to her. I don't want to love, I never wanted to love again, but I do love. I love Madeleine…she fills my life with light…God knows that I'll suffer for it…but there's nothing I can do to stop it. I might just as well try and hold back the wind."

Behind the bushes Madeleine grinned. There! It was true! She was right! Her heart swelled with hope. If he loved her too, then they would find a way.

Nancy touched Ryan's hand in sympathy. "Then the good Lord in heaven save us all!" She grimaced, "I don't know why the Mistress has taken against you."

"I've seen it before - that 'look' - not being good enough…"

"Not good enough? But your *true* father…"

"Hush Nancy - don't speak of it, please."

"But if the Mistress knew…"

"If she knew who my father really was do you think it would make her accept me? It wouldn't. She'd use the circumstances of my birth against me. She'd betray me to them. I have my freedom and I want to keep it."

"But you told me your freedom depended on you not staying too long here."

"That may be true, but maybe they have forgotten about me by now. All the more reason that Margaret can't know who I really am, so that she can't remind them."

Now Madeleine was really intrigued. She couldn't understand

what they were talking about.

Nancy said, "Very well…I'll help you any way I can, though God preserve us, we'll all pay when the Mistress finds out…as she *will*."

"I can be happy just being near Madeleine. If I don't take it any further, there will be nothing for the Mistress to find out. I'm bound here, not by chains maybe, but by something stronger…whatever fate decrees."

CHAPTER SEVEN

Now that she knew Ryan loved her, Madeleine puzzled over the problem of how to make him admit it, for *she* could not be happy just being near *him*! Finally she thought of a plan that she was sure would work. As winter waned, she waited impatiently until the right set of circumstances came along. The days passed so slowly until at long last the scene could be set. She'd been waiting for a day when Ryan was working in the fields alone, and out of sight of the house, and finally the day came. She secretly saddled a horse, and rode towards where Ryan was working. She passed him not one hundred paces away, but he gave no sign that he'd seen her. He didn't look up from his work at all. She almost doubted her heart.

She rode the mare out of Ryan's sight, looking back to see if she could catch him watching her secretly, but no, he kept his gaze firmly on the ground he was tending. Once she was well out of sight she dismounted from the mare, turned her back towards home and picking up a branch from the track, she screamed out and shook it at the horse until she swerved away in fright and fled back the way they had come.

Quickly, Madeleine arranged the scene. She dropped face-down to the ground, arms outstretched, motionless, and waited. She didn't dare look up to see if her ruse was working. She couldn't risk Ryan realising she wasn't really hurt before he showed her his true feelings. It was a cruel trick, and she felt a bit ashamed of herself, but she couldn't go on the way they had been any longer. She didn't hear him coming on the soft track until he was almost upon her.

As he drew near enough for her to hear his pounding feet, she heard him cry, breathlessly, "Oh Mother of God, no!" He crashed to the ground beside her. He touched her gently, as if afraid of being too rough. He carefully felt her arms and legs to see if any bones were broken. After he'd tenderly felt her skull, and had started to stroke the side of her face, Madeleine couldn't contain herself any longer. She opened her eyes.

"Oh thank God, thank God," he breathed. Then he gathered her into his arms and sat there rocking her back and forth, his relieved breath sobbing in his throat.

She had her answer. She felt a bit mean to have scared him, but she'd had no choice. After a while Ryan helped her to her feet. Madeleine pretended to be dazed, although she was really so happy that she could have turned cartwheels. As they walked back to the house, Ryan tried desperately to distance himself from her again, frantically backing off, but Madeleine wasn't fooled for a second.

After dark, Madeleine crept to the barn doors again, and this time Ryan didn't pretend to be asleep. He heard the door creak slightly and knew it was her. He sat up the instant she walked inside. She stood quietly for a moment looking down at him on the straw, her eyebrows raised slightly, and her eyes clearly showed that this time she wanted the truth. He looked at her. At the way the moon's light lit her from behind, making a silhouette of her slim body. At her eyes, glowing with love and need for *him*. The love and need she obviously felt for him was more seductive than anything he had ever known. He felt his blood rise and didn't know what to do to stop the inevitable.

After what seemed like minutes of contemplative and awkward silence between them, which was really probably only seconds, Ryan found some words, "Madeleine, you make this so difficult. You can't be found here. What do you want of me?"

She dropped to her knees beside him in the straw. "Nothing *of* you. *Just* you. All I ever wanted was you, to be beside you, tonight and every night."

"Oh God help me," he whispered. "What am I to do?" He wrenched his eyes away from Madeleine's face, in turmoil. He wouldn't, he couldn't, look at her. His mind and his blood raced. He should walk away, he knew he should. He should move on like he always had before, but the thought of wandering alone, when he could stay with someone who truly loved him…the thought of being without her was worse than death. There was only one answer.

After a few silent moments, while she waited, anxiety painted on her face, he drew a deep shuddering breath. It was over. He could not resist walking into the fire any longer. Still facing away from her, he reached out to her with one hand. Madeleine took it in hers and he tugged her so that she fell down into his arms. He held her close, but he still had his eyes shut tight, fighting another inner battle, his breathing heavy. They would burn; they would both burn together, if he went any further. He could feel her heart drumming alongside his own. Burn together, or live apart? That would not be living. With a long sigh of surrender, he opened his eyes, and the love there was plain to see. Then at last he kissed her. He felt like he was drowning, but he didn't and couldn't care. He made no move to be more intimate, but he continued to kiss her, his arms wrapping her tightly against him, and for some while that was enough for him. But his body started to flood with a tide of passion that he couldn't control. He knew that she would have lain there all night, answering his every need had he let her. But it would have been fatally foolish. Had she become pregnant, then that new life would have been *his* immediate death warrant.

After a while he stopped kissing her and stared into her eyes, a bare inch from his. They were bright and yet mysterious, and he knew that she felt the same reckless passion he did.

"You must go now," he breathed, making no attempt to release her. "I can't do this anymore. Please go, while I can still let you." Her being there, with him naked under his blanket, and nothing else between them but her cotton nightgown, was impossible for him. She seemed to understand, kissing him lightly one last time, but he didn't allow himself to respond. When she looked back at him from the doorway he was flat out on the straw again, his arm covering his eyes, his fist clenched, struggling to control his emotions, and knowing that he had taken a step that would be impossible to retreat from.

What Madeleine didn't know, as she walked across the yard to the kitchen door, was that she was being watched. Gossip among the servants had reached Margaret. If Madeleine had looked up, she'd probably have noticed the twitch of curtains from her stepmother and father's bedchamber window. If she hadn't been deafened by her own heartbeat, she might have heard the quiet 'snick' of the window closing. The next day she eventually guessed they knew about her night visit to Ryan because of the chilly atmosphere and the unspoken accusations that filled the air. Every time she looked Margaret's way, she could feel cold waves of disapproval streaming from her stepmother.

The following night Madeleine eavesdropped outside her parents' bedroom door. She was sure that they would be plotting some way to get rid of Ryan, and she wanted to be able to warn him. Sure enough they were discussing what would turn out to be a terrible mistake. They were talking about offering Ryan a large sum of money if he'd leave. Madeleine listened as they made their dark plans, wondering how they could have ignored her needs and feelings so easily. She had no doubt that Ryan would refuse them.

As Madeleine crept up to her parents' bedroom door and quietly pressed her ear against it, Margaret was speaking, "Edwin! I tell you that Irishman is about to ruin your daughter!"

Edwin answered her, "I think you're over-reacting, my dear..."

"Over-reacting? He's already bedded serving wenches from the neighbouring estate!"

"He's a young man, just doing what young men do...with those who are willing...but not Madeleine...he won't..."

"He won't? Won't! Are you mad? Of *course* he *will* if he thinks he can get away with it! She was down there, with him, last night, alone! Thank God I was warned about this! If you let this go on, Pennington won't marry her and we'll be disgraced! Do as I say! It's the only way! You'll have to pay him off!"

"Margaret, please calm down my dear. He seems to feel something quite genuine for Madeleine, and she is besotted. Perhaps their love is real."

"That vagabond! That...that...! What would someone like that know about love? What use is love anyway? I want the alliance with Pennington, not for myself, for the family! Don't you see? Your daughter must learn to listen to her betters. You've spoiled her! They must be parted. Buy him off!"

"Very well my dear, I'll settle it."

"And if he won't be bought, then he'll learn not to challenge me! He'll be sorry if he denies me!"

Madeleine heard the faint jingle of coins as her father collected a money pouch from his dresser, and then he came out into the hallway, and she had to hide from him.

Edwin went straight to the barn to make his demands, with Madeleine sneaking along behind him, unable to give Ryan any warning after all. She had to hide deep in the shadows of the hallway until her father appeared, then she followed him across the yard. She watched the whole encounter from just outside the barn, her eye at the crack of the doors. She was furious with her father, and curious to see how Ryan would react.

Ryan had already bedded down for the night, and he sat up, surprised, when Edwin walked in. He got to his feet as Edwin approached him, wrapping the rug about himself as he stood.

The two men regarded each other silently for a moment, and then Ryan spoke.

"You have something to say?" he asked.

In answer Edwin threw the pouch of money to the straw at Ryan's bare feet. Madeleine stared in interest. She had never seen Ryan's bare feet before. She had often spied on Ryan as he washed in the yard, her eyes distracted by the sight of his bare chest and thighs. That night, however, she was almost distracted with more than she'd bargained for. Refusing to be intimidated by his situation, Ryan calmly dropped the rug, which had been maintaining his dignity, to the floor, with no show of embarrassment, and stooped unhurriedly to pull on his breeches. Fortunately for Madeleine's innocence, but sadly for her inquisitive eyes, Edwin chose that very moment to step into her line of vision, blocking Ryan's nakedness from her sight.

"What's this for?" Ryan asked, pointing at the pouch but making no attempt to pick it up.

"It's for you to make a new start," Edwin answered.

"Very generous."

"There is however, a condition."

"I thought there might be."

"This new start must be far from this place," Edwin announced.

"And far from Madeleine?" Ryan asked.

"That also."

"*No.*" Ryan's voice when he said that one word was quiet, but so firm that Madeleine's heart felt a surge of joy. The door of Ryan's heart had been opened, and now it was firmly closed, holding his love for her deep inside it. There were no more doubts and no turning back, ever.

"I haven't made the situation clear." Edwin continued, "You're not being given a choice. You can either leave here in peace with this wealth, which to you will be more money than you will ever see again or…"

"Or what?" Ryan's voice had grown very cold.

"You'll either leave this house and my daughter immediately; or steps will be taken to make sure that you leave here in a very sorry state, and as penniless as you came. But either way you *will* choose to leave, I promise you."

"You're mistaken. Just because you're wealthy, it doesn't mean that you own me. I don't and will never choose to leave here unless Madeleine leaves with me. Her choice can only be her own."

"She's but a child - you toy with her."

"No! You give her no credit. She's not to be toyed with; she's full-grown. And she's…" Ryan paused, and then smiled a smile of implication, "…she's *mine.*

The response was predictably furious, "Yours! I'll see you dead before she's yours! Or are you saying that you've already ruined her?"

"I've not bedded her, if that's what you ask."

"Then it's not too late. Now, will you leave, in good health? Or must we take action to see that you leave?"

"I'll not leave without her."

"Believe me; you'll come to bitterly regret your defiance of us in this matter."

"I may come to pay for this defiance, if your threats are real, but regret it? No. Whatever you do I'll still be here. I love your daughter as she loves me, and I'll never leave her." He picked up the pouch and thrust it into Edwin's hands. "This merely proves how much she's worth to you, not how much you love her. It's a pity you don't love her as much as I do."

Edwin looked full of rage, but left the barn in silence. Ryan remained where he was, his eyes sparkling with equal fury.

Madeleine came out of hiding, and Ryan was upset when he realised that she'd overheard the whole conversation. He pulled her to him fiercely, and she clung to him with the same need, her hands stroking the bare skin of his back.

Finally, Ryan stepped away from her, "I didn't want it to be like this! Not to tear you from your family." He paced for a few moments and then stopped, his eyes fixed on Madeleine. He knew without doubt that what he was about to do would bring terrible consequences, but his fate was undeniable. He dropped to his knees at her feet, his reckless decision made. He took one of her hands in his. "When I came here, I found what I never thought I wanted. I found someone I cared about and someone who cared about me. I swore I'd never love anyone again, but love had other ideas. I've nothing to offer you except my body and soul, and if you marry me, you'll lose the love of your family and it's so much for you to give up." He paused, looking intensely into her eyes, "I only swear that I love you, and I believe I've loved you for *all* time."

Madeleine answered, smiling, "I don't need anything more in this world than you forever beside me. To be your wife is all I'll ever want."

"I don't know if you understand the consequences of this night…I do…but this time I'll follow my heart, and they won't stop me. I'll take my chances, and it will be worth it…" She never heard his last quiet whisper, "For however long…" he said.

Madeleine rushed to share her joyous news with Nancy in the kitchen, but if she expected Nancy to share her happiness, she was disappointed.

Nancy chastised her immediately, "Don't you know the danger you've put him in child?"

"Father won't harm him, not now he knows how much we are in love!"

"How little you know…" Nancy said, sadly.

"It'll be all right - our love's so strong. I can't imagine being without him now. I'd die."

"That may be true but I'm very afraid for you both."

Nancy loved both the young people as if they were her own children. Since the death of her husband, Tom, many years since, she had been quite lonely. When Rebecca had died, she felt as if Madeleine looked to her for a mother. When Edwin moved his new wife and his young daughter to the new house, it had given Nancy a new lease of life. And when she had seen how unhappy Madeleine was, she was only too pleased to step in again as a mother-figure to her. When Ryan had appeared on the scene, she had fallen for his blue eyes as quickly as Madeleine had. He was an upstanding young man as far as she was concerned, and it had been a puzzle to her that Margaret took against him so badly at first sight. She quickly came to realise that Margaret's worst nightmare would be her step-daughter falling for one such as him. That wouldn't fit in with her plans at all. Knowing that, she was terrified now for both of them.

By the next morning Ryan's behaviour changed towards Madeleine. Having taken the fatal step, he was free and light-hearted. Every time they looked at each other they smiled. They were openly affectionate and felt the need to touch each other often, in tender ways that could not be misconstrued by spying eyes as anything other than loving. Without doubt his displays of affection drove Margaret to desperate and despicable lengths. Two days later Ryan was to reap the whirlwind of her desperation.

CHAPTER EIGHT

Margaret and Edwin were mystified, enraged and horror-stricken that Ryan had refused the bribe. They couldn't understand it all. He had been offered more money that he could ever have seen in his lifetime. It should have been an irresistible offer to him. By refusing a fair offer he deserved everything that was going to come to him. Desperate times called for desperate measures. He couldn't be allowed to get away with defying them. He had to go, and quickly. They discussed the situation deep into the night, searching for a solution. The decision they came to was to drive Madeleine even further away from them, and ever closer to Ryan.

The town blacksmith, Mr Taylor, had made a new, heavy wrought iron gate for the house, and it gave them the opportunity they'd been looking for. They sent Ryan, alone, down to fetch it, knowing that he would take the short-cut down the green lane. Timing things carefully, they arranged for Madeleine to be tied up with a string of chores in the house, so that she could not go with him. The hired thugs would do the rest.

Making Ryan bring the heavy gate back to the house alone had been a clever ploy on Margaret and Edwin's part. His carrying the unwieldy object was what helped the men they had hired to surprise him. He was taking his usual shortcut across the lane at the back of the village, and was so occupied with manhandling the gate over the hedge that he did not see the stealthy figures skulking in the shadows. The gate clanged to the ground on the other side of the hedge and he bent to pick it up. That was when he saw movement out of the corner of his eye and he straightened hurriedly again, stepping away from the gate to avoid being tripped by it should he need to move quickly. He had a very unsettling feeling about the two men who were then approaching him.

"Excuse me, good sir," one spoke, his manner well out of keeping with his appearance. "Is this the right road for Hambledon?"

In the meantime, indoors, Madeleine was growing suspicious. Like a dutiful daughter she had started to obey Margaret's instructions, but after she was left by herself, she started to realise that the chores were in no way as urgent as she had been told. Something was going on. Could the chores be a diversion? She suddenly felt knives of fear drive right through her and knew for certain that Ryan was unknowingly walking into some terrible danger. She fled the house as if on wings.

The man's question didn't put Ryan off guard, but increased his caution. He took two steps back, ready to flee or fight as circumstances dictated. But the steps back were halted as he realised that someone was behind him. Ryan turned to assess the new danger and there stood two more men, grinning nastily. And worse yet, two more men emerged from the shadows. He was surrounded. Six of them now and every one looking like the spawn of the devil. Ryan's heart began to race, though he gave no outward sign. He was sure they would be on him like a pack of wolves at the first sign of weakness. The men started to circle him, all pretence gone now.

"What is it that you want?" Ryan asked, holding his voice steady.

"Just a little entertainment," said one.

"Of course," another chuckled, "you may not find it entertaining."

From the third, "But we will earn our pay, just the same."

"And we enjoy our work," said the next.

"Take a great pride in a job well done," came from the fifth man.

The sixth man said nothing but stepped forwards and shoved Ryan in the chest, trying to unbalance him. But Ryan was planted like a tree, and did not move.

The sixth man spoke, "Now be sensible and give us no trouble and it will be over quickly. The end is inevitable, and any hurt you inflict on us will only serve you worse in the end. Give us trouble, and we will enjoy our work all the more, for we have plenty of time." He laughed, and the others laughed too.

Ryan swallowed. His mouth was dry, and a sour taste filled his throat. He had faced this kind of threat before but not against six. He knew that one way or another he was going to be badly hurt and the knowledge was very unpleasant. At that moment Madeleine rushed into the lane, and stopped short as the nightmare scene greeted her. Her appearance made things even worse for Ryan, because he could not hope to protect her against six.

He tried to make her leave, calling to her, "Madeleine, run! Back to the house!" She didn't move, and sensing her fury, he tried again, "Madeleine! Stay back! There's nothing you can do here."

In response, Madeleine reached down and grabbed up a hefty branch from the grass. Screaming like a banshee, she rushed at one of the men and clouted him over the head. He fell to the ground, stunned. Quick to react now that there was no turning back, Ryan smacked a fist into one attacker's face so that he dropped to the ground as if pole-axed. But now the men divided their attention. Two ran at Madeleine and two at Ryan. His dismay at the attack on Madeleine lent fury to his strength and, wanting to help her, he quickly threw one of his attackers to the ground, bloodied.

A well-aimed kick caused the second man to stumble over the gate that still lay where it had fallen, and Ryan's fist was already swinging towards his face when the shout of, "Stop! If you care for this girl, stop!" came from the men's leader. He and another man had hold of Madeleine's arms.

She struggled with the men, and tried to tell Ryan that she would not be harmed. "No!" she cried desperately, "They won't dare! Don't listen to him!"

But the other three men were already scrambling to their feet, and Ryan knew his chance was gone. Coupled with that, the sight of the two ruffians' hands on Madeleine conjured up visions too awful to contemplate, so he stopped, his hand frozen into a fist.

"That's better," the leader said, "Now you…" he pointed a grimy finger in Ryan's direction, "…will take your just punishment, with no resistance, or…" He pointed back at Madeleine. "…this fine lady will accompany us back to our lodgings to repay us for our trouble."

Ryan wouldn't risk it. There was no choice. He sighed deeply, his breath snorting from his nostrils. As heartily sick as he was at having his every move dictated by rich folk, there seemed to be no escape from it, and no escape either for what was coming. Meeting Madeleine's eyes across the lane he shook his head, and then dropped his arms to his sides in mute surrender. Two men continued to hold Madeleine fast as she screamed and fought.

One of the men holding her hissed in her ear, "Don't worry my pretty, we will not kill him. Not quite."

The two men Ryan had knocked down pounced on him vengefully. His fists clenched involuntarily, his arm muscles tensing as two of the men took hold of him. Obviously feeling the potential there for further harm to them, the men twisted his arms behind his back, their fingers digging fiercely into the skin of his forearms as they tightened their grip to prevent any resistance. But he didn't dare resist, in case they harmed Madeleine. He tried not to show his fear, although only a fool would not feel any. A third man got to his feet and strutted cockily up to him. Ryan sneered in his face, though his chest was tight and his stomach knotted. The first punch felt like a hammer blow to his ribs, and Ryan grunted as the wind was knocked out of him. Then the man hit him in the mouth, and he tasted salty blood. Soon he could not breathe for the blows to his body, and everything went black.

Ryan was dragged unwillingly from the merciful darkness by a sudden excruciating pain in his back. Light seeped into his eyes and he realised he was lying on the road, dust filling his mouth, and that he had been kicked. A hand snatched at his hair and pulled his head up.

Foul breath puffed into his face and a voice heard through a dizzying fog said, "Last chance lad. Do you swear to leave this place and never return?"

His mouth felt swollen and unresponsive but Ryan managed to utter, "No. I do not," knowing that it would bring further punishment, but unable to deny himself.

Madeleine was crying and screaming, begging the men to stop. They seemed pleased to be refused by Ryan, and they laughed and started to kick him again, each one eager for his turn. Ryan twisted and turned on the ground but was not able to avoid the blows. Instinct drove him to his hands and knees but a kick to his abdomen tossed him over on his side once more. The men began to taunt him. They were excited and out of control.

"Come on then! Get up! Get up!" they yelled at him. "Crawl! On yer belly!"

He did try to get up again; something drove him to keep trying. But it was useless. The men ran around, competing for the best position to kick him again. Ryan was gasping for breath, as again and again he was winded by a kick, and his strength was fading fast. The men were in blood-lust and he knew he was going to die.

Distantly, he heard Madeleine screaming, "Stop, stop, you said you wouldn't kill him!" Her voice broke into sobs.

Everything stopped when the leader shouted, "She's right. We weren't to kill him! Stop now!" The men gradually obeyed him, one by one, tearing themselves from their dark place with obvious effort. "However," he continued, "We were to prevent him taking delight with a woman!"

Ryan's body was almost numb to the pain, and he had allowed himself to drift away. But when a boot hit him squarely between his legs, the worst pain he had ever known blazed through his entire body, bringing him back to awareness, so that he cried out in agony. The rest was nothing compared to this. It was as if every nerve ending in his body was centred in his groin and a wave of nausea overwhelmed him. He curled up reflexively, gasping and retching.

The man walked over to Ryan and leaned down, saying the words, "Now you *will* choose to leave!"

Ryan had no answer, for he could not speak.

He saw their feet retreating, and then Madeleine was there beside him. Still he couldn't speak, and torrents of pain clouded his mind. Madeleine was crying out his name. In response, he tried to get up but the pain took his strength and his legs wouldn't obey him. Madeleine took his arm and tried to pull him up, but he couldn't bear to be moved. He found his voice and begged her to leave him alone.

He didn't know how long it might be until he could bear to move, but for a while he just needed to be still, for every muscle twitch sent fresh bolts of pain rippling through him.

Finally she left him, and then after a while she came back with two workmen. They tried to be careful, but the journey back to the barn was a seemingly unending haze of hurting. When they lay him on the straw, he was pathetically grateful, just for the cessation of movement. Madeleine had fetched Nancy, and she tried to help him though it was hard for him to let her. It was better when she sent Madeleine away because the anguish on her face and her cries made him feel even worse. At last the pain eased to a level that was bearable but at any threat of movement his protesting torn muscles and bruised innards shattered him with terrible cramps. It was going to be a very long night.

Nancy didn't let Madeleine to go back to him until she'd tended all his injuries, and he was decently covered with his blanket, looking a little less drawn. But as she let Madeleine back in, she confided some news to her in a whisper that turned the girl's soul to ice.

"The blackness of his skin shows that there is bleeding deep within his body. I can't do any more for him, and the morning will tell if he'll live."

Madeleine's heart stuttered and she almost passed out at the words, waves of dread slamming into her heart, but she tried not to let Ryan see. She was determined that just for once she'd be the strong one, for his sake. She sat with Ryan all through the night, holding him when he could let her, and crying fresh tears whenever a new jolt of pain shook him. It seemed that the night was to be eternal.

Finally the sun started to rise, and Ryan seemed to pass into a normal sleep so that Nancy said she believed that he would survive. Relief swept through Madeleine's being. Her parents didn't know how close they came during that night to harm at their daughter's hands. And at ten o' clock in the morning Margaret appeared at the barn door. Madeleine was on her feet in an instant, incandescent with rage, ready to defend Ryan with her life.

"What do you want here?" she almost screamed.

"Madeleine, you've been out here all night. We are afraid for your reputation."

"Fear not for my reputation," she replied, "Fear more for your own safety."

"My dear child…" Margaret tried to soothe her, "…you're overwrought. What's happened?"

Even as she spoke, Margaret was trying to step around Madeleine so that she could see more of Ryan, and the girl knew then that her stepmother had come to gloat over the results of her paid thugs' actions. Madeleine stepped towards her threateningly, and her eyes looked straight into Margaret's soul, appalled at the hatred she saw carved deeply there. Margaret saw inside Madeleine's mind too, and something she saw written there caused her to drop her gaze and hurriedly leave the barn.

Ryan had been disturbed by all the shouting and he had his eyes open, although he wasn't yet strong enough to sit up. But at least he looked alive.

"My dear…" Nancy began, "…it becomes apparent to me…and I have to say…"

"Don't worry Nancy. Do you think I don't know who's responsible for this cowardly act?" She turned to Ryan, "All I ask you is whether you want to leave me now? I couldn't blame you if you did."

"I'll be here for as long as you want me," he answered firmly.

"Then please excuse me." Madeleine looked back at him and the suffering burning in his eyes inflamed her anger further. She left the barn.

She confronted her parents in the drawing room, giving them no chance to speak first, saying, "I won't waste my breath accusing you because I know you'll deny all blame. However, I'll tell you this. I know what you've done. If any further harm comes to Ryan then you had best do the same to me, for I swear by God, I will kill anyone who harms him again. Don't you yet understand, Father, what you do to him you also do to me? If you thought to bully him into leaving me, where your bribery failed; then you've failed again. I also tell you this: I love Ryan more than life itself and, had you succeeded in driving him away, then my life would have meant nothing, and I would have ended it."

With this she turned and left the sight of their startled faces. She went back to the barn, and found Ryan lying there once more in a peaceful sleep. She sat beside him and pressed one of his hands between both of hers, kissing it tenderly.

CHAPTER NINE

As Ryan's health improved over the next few weeks, Madeleine felt that they should get married as soon as possible, because she thought that only then would Ryan be safe from her parents. Surely, once she'd been made truly his in the eyes of God, then no-one else would want her. Her parents would stop trying to get rid of him so that they could marry her off to someone else.

Ryan and Madeleine sat up at night planning their wedding. As soon as arrangements could be made they would journey to the Abbey church, in the village of Middleton. It was a long ride away but Ryan said that it was so beautiful that he knew Madeleine would love it. At that time it was not being used as a church, so a secret ceremony wouldn't be too hard to achieve. In those times, the giving and receiving of a ring in front of witnesses was all that was required to make a solemn and legal binding.

The night before Ryan and Madeleine were to leave to be married, Madeleine couldn't sleep. She decided to go down to the kitchen because Nancy's kind sister, Sarah, was visiting the house, and they were always good company. They were the only ones who knew about the proposed marriage, and so they were the only ones she could talk to. As she thought, the two sisters were warming themselves, sitting in front of the kitchen fire, cradling a goblet of wine each. The big fire was now all cosy embers, turning the whole room into a comforting pink and amber cave, as the sunset colours reflected off the lime plaster walls.

After a while the conversation took turn that puzzled Madeleine.

With a knowing wink at Nancy, Sarah spoke, "Beware, my lady, of a well-endowed man for he may be impatient with you and cause you pain."

"Whatever do you mean?" Madeleine asked her, bewilderment on her face.

Sarah turned a little pink in the cheeks, and her reply confused Madeleine even more. "Well, he might be careless of your sensibilities. He might force his way with you and you might not be able to accommodate him without discomfort."

Madeleine didn't understand at all. Was Sarah referring to Ryan's wealth or his property when she spoke of a man being well endowed? In any case Madeleine knew this didn't apply to him, because Ryan had neither wealth nor property. When she pointed this out, both older women showed signs of great amusement and laughed at her until she became quite angry.

Finally Nancy patted Madeleine's knee comfortingly, "Don't concern yourself my love," she advised. "Ryan is a gentle and considerate man, and I know he'll take good care not to hurt you, and he will, I'm sure, see to it that you are made...content." This time it was Nancy who winked at Sarah, and both women collapsed into gales of laughter.

Madeleine couldn't imagine Ryan ever hurting her in any way, and so she decided it was nothing but a foolish joke on the sisters' parts. She decided to ignore their laughter. She intended to go back to her bed, but almost without thinking, she found herself standing outside the barn doors. She opened one just a tiny crack, enough to see through. She had decided not to wake Ryan if he was asleep. He wasn't. He was sitting up in his makeshift bed, his knees bent in front of him, arms resting on them on top of the blanket that covered him. He patted the place at his side, inviting her to join him. When she reached his side she was surprised to see a second blanket laid out next to his, in anticipation of her arrival. It was quite obvious that he'd been expecting her to come. Neither of them spoke, because no words were needed. Madeleine crawled under the blanket Ryan had put out for her, and turned on her side to face him. He snuggled down under his own blanket.

Madeleine started to tell him about the curious conversation she'd shared with Sarah and Nancy, saying, "They said you are well-endowed and I told them that I know you are not!"

Ryan's mouth began to twitch in amusement, though he tried to hide it, screwing his mouth up to disguise the smile. He took in Madeleine's totally puzzled and rather hurt expression and tried to be serious, but a broad grin forced itself onto his face. Madeleine frowned at him, and her eyes started to fill with tears.

Ryan repented immediately, "Don't worry, my love. You're right, I'd never hurt you. They were just joking. You'll never have anything to fear from me. I'll explain it all to you when we're wed and you'll understand." But he was still smiling as he reached out and took her hand in his.

Thinking about the conversation she had overheard between Ryan and Nancy concerning Ryan's family, Madeleine put out her hand and touched the ring that hung on a cord around his neck, "Will you be wearing this as a sign of our vows? Was it your father's?"

"Why do you ask?" he said.

She didn't want to confess that she'd eavesdropped on him and Nancy, so she couldn't ask any further questions, and just said, "Just something I wondered."

"Yes, I'll wear it."

"Where did it come from?"

"I'll tell you everything, but another time."

Their eyes locked in an embrace, and they gazed ever more sleepily at each other, until they finally drifted to sleep. Ryan had been pleased that Madeleine had brought him laughter, because he had been brooding about the inevitable consequences of their elopement.

The first thing Madeleine saw when she woke in the morning was that Ryan was awake and was watching her. She knew right then that the thing she most longed for in the whole world was to wake up to that sight every day for the rest of her life.

The next day, on 27 April 1638, the two of them rode for hours to reach their destination. Ryan knew of the church from when he'd lived and worked on a farm in the village of Charlton Marshall, not far away from it. He took Madeleine to the farm first. The farmer's family were pleased to see them, especially the daughter, Marian. Madeleine was a little jealous of the familiarity with which the girl greeted Ryan, throwing her arms around him and kissing him on the mouth. Marian was very pretty, plump, with dark, curly hair, brown eyes and a very red mouth. Ryan stepped away from Marian and put his arm possessively around Madeleine, leaving no room for misinterpretation. Marian glared at Madeleine a bit scornfully, but Madeleine paid her no more attention. If she envied her Ryan, then no-one could blame her.

Later, Ryan left Madeleine at the farm, and disappeared in the direction of the Abbey. He was gone all evening, and half the night. The farmer had allowed them the use of his hay barn for the night, and Madeleine was already asleep there when Ryan came back. She woke up briefly in her makeshift bed of hay as he flopped down beside her in exhaustion. Within seconds they were both fast asleep.

They were woken at dawn by the farmer coming into the barn to feed his stock. Ryan seemed very excited. Madeleine had been afraid that he'd involved Nancy in some way, and might be risking her position in the household, but all Nancy had done was to give him her wedding ring for Madeleine to use. Her husband had been long dead, but Madeleine was very touched by Nancy's sacrifice, because the ring was still precious to her. They both wished that their friend could have been at the wedding, but it would have been impossible to keep her absence from the house a secret.

They didn't have anything special to wear for the wedding, and Ryan was a bit dusty after his mysterious secret labours. They brushed him down as much as possible and Madeleine wove a crown for her hair out of spring flowers wrapped around a circlet made from a hazel wand. They rode to the Abbey church, and arrived there at eight o' clock.

A man Madeleine had never seen before arrived on horseback, breathless, and Ryan introduced his friend to Madeleine. His name was Jared, and he'd ridden many miles to be a witness to Ryan's marriage. Jared was of stocky build, with shoulder length blond hair, and was a friend of Ryan's from the village.

Jared was not the type of man that Margaret would have ever allowed in the house or grounds, and this was why Madeleine had never seen him before. Jared was a homosexual, and although at the turn of the century, King James VI of Scotland had made a nonsense of the previous Queen's 'anti-homosex' by openly taking George Villiers for his permanent intimate companion, there were still some who were prejudiced against such people, and Margaret, predictably, was one of them. It was also typical of Ryan that he would not hold any kind of prejudice.

Madeleine was stunned when she saw the inside of the church. She didn't know how he could possibly have done it, but Ryan had filled the area around the altar with wild flowers, bunches and bunches of them, in yellow and blue. There were over fifty candles, in stone sconces, burning in a half circle around the altar itself. She turned to him, her eyes pricking with tears; loving him with such intensely that it almost hurt. They made their way under the vaulted ceiling to the altar, where there stood a man of the clergy, who had agreed to perform the ceremony. He looked very nervous and kept glancing at the church door anxiously. Jared and the farmer and his family were gathered around. The ceremony was short, to avoid someone finding them there, but perfect even so.

The church looked like a magic cave, with the flickering pools created by the candles, and the blue and yellow of all the flowers, as they made their vows.

Madeleine spoke first, "No-one owns me, and therefore no-one can give me. I give myself to you, with no part held back. You'll know every part of me, even to my soul. I'll never deceive you, and I'll never have a secret from you. I'll love you forever, for I can't help myself."

Ryan replied, "I'll defend you with my body, and I'll love you with my soul. I'll never deceive you, and I'll never leave you while I still breathe. I'll protect you from all others, even unto laying down my life at your feet. My life is yours for the taking."

Madeleine didn't flinch when Marian took her opportunity to kiss Ryan again. He and Jared joked together for a while, but then Ryan's friend and witness had to leave to attend some urgent family matters.

It seemed that he had been summoned home to the family farm because his sister was in trouble.

Ryan and Jared clasped hands before they parted, and Madeleine never heard Ryan's whispered words, "Jared, if anything happens to me…"

Jared's reply was equally covert, "I'll look after her, don't worry my friend." With that he sketched a wave to the rest of the party, swung his leg over his horse, and set off at a gallop for the countryside of the Welsh borders.

CHAPTER TEN

The talk of Jared's family brought Ryan and Madeleine back to reality, and with trepidation, they set off immediately to face the trouble they knew would inevitably be waiting for them at home. Madeleine hoped that her stepmother and father might accept the deed once it was done. They both knew that Edwin and Margaret would have been concerned when the couple hadn't returned home the previous evening, and thought they might have guessed what was going on. They were right, and Madeleine was about to have a lesson in how deeply she had displeased her parents.

They entered the house, and stood quietly in the hallway. Both of them were nervous. Madeleine twisted her ring round and round on her finger.

Ryan's hand rested on her shoulder, and squeezed comfortingly. "This could go very hard on you. Are you sure we've done the right thing? Maybe we shouldn't have come back here…"

She looked at the ring and smiled, "I feel more right at this moment than I've ever felt before. They'll see, and they'll have to accept our love now that we're married." She walked ahead of Ryan towards the drawing room door. She knew he wasn't so sure, and stopped at the door and looked back at him. Ryan shook his head, doubt on his face, but he followed her.

Margaret leapt to her feet when Madeleine and Ryan came in. Edwin stood at the fireplace. He looked drawn and ill, as if Margaret had been nagging him. The woman was scarlet with pent up rage, and she marched over to Ryan and pushed with both hands against his chest in fury, trying to make him move from Madeleine's side.

Then she turned her back on him, and shouted at his new wife.

"Madeleine! What have you done?"

She held out her hand, "Ryan and I are wed."

"No!" Margaret screamed in fury. She clutched Madeleine's outstretched hand, trying to pull the ring off. Madeleine snatched her hand back, fisted.

"Let go! No-one will ever take the ring unless it is from my cold dead body!"

Margaret screamed at her, "You idiot child! You've been promised to Joseph Pennington, that good man of London, for years. Do you understand what you've given up?" She pointed at Ryan, "For this!"

"*I've* given up nothing. *You've* lost the prestige of having the Pennington name associated with your family. You'll miss your stepdaughter becoming the heir to a fortune."

"You've missed being married to security!" Margaret insisted.

"No. I've escaped being tied to an old man for whom I have no use! I'm wed to the only man I'll ever love! *You* marry for security. *I* marry for love!"

"Love! What is love?" Her mouth made a moue of disgust.

Madeleine showed her anger in return, "You'll never know! You married father for *money,* and you'll *never* replace my real mother!"

Margaret lost control and drew back her hand to slap Madeleine in the face. Ryan stepped forward quickly and grasped her wrist.

With a single quiet word, "*No,*" he pushed her arm down.

She snatched her hand away, and turned to face him with undisguised disgust on her face, her eyes big with indignation. "You dare to lay hands on me! You insolent scoundrel! Know this; you will *never* be a son to me!"

Ryan couldn't help but smile at the absurdity of this comment, "A son to *you?* I will never be desperate enough to want it."

The smile, and the words, drove Margaret insane. She brought her arm swinging round and slapped Ryan on the face as hard as she could. This time he didn't try to stop her, but stood unmoving as the shape of her splayed fingers flamed red on his cheek. His eyes met hers steadily, contemptuously, until she was forced to look away.

Finally she shouted again, "Neither of you will ever set foot in this house again!"

At last, finally, Edwin spoke, "Margaret, I won't have my only child rendered homeless like some common waif."

"She doesn't deserve to be your daughter!"

"Nevertheless," he answered firmly, "She *is* my daughter. She is my *blood.*"

Margaret subsided slightly at this slightly threatening comment. "What of him?" she demanded.

Madeleine spoke up quickly, "If Ryan…if my husband leaves, then I leave with him, right now, and forever! Make no mistake Father!"

"You may both stay, for the moment." Edwin may have been ailing and weak, but he showed that he still had authority over Margaret when he really chose to use it.

"Very well," Margaret conceded grudgingly, having little choice, "Your father shows more mercy than you deserve. But I insist that from this day, until the day when you repent your mistake, you'll only have access to your bedchamber and the servants' areas. You've disgraced this family, and you no longer deserve to be accepted as a part of it." She turned to Ryan again, "As for you. You'll have no more privileges in this house than the lowest servant.

If you imagined that by disgracing our daughter, you'd become accepted into this family, you're mistaken. Madeleine, you are but a foolish child, and after some time in *his* company, you'll soon come to your senses. In the meantime, you will move all your belongings into one of the servants' rooms in the new wing. That way you can use the back stairs, and I won't have to see either one of you!" She looked to Edwin angrily, daring him to try and deny her further, and he nodded his assent to her wishes. Madeleine swept from the room with her small triumph, and Ryan followed her.

They went to the kitchen to share their joy, and their anger, with Nancy.

"They'll never change," Madeleine declared, "They still don't accept my feelings."

"They never will," Nancy agreed, sadly.

"Come," said Ryan, "No sad faces. This is the happiest day of *my* life at least!" He grinned mischievously.

The couple went upstairs to Madeleine's bedroom and collected all her things, carrying them down the main stairs and into the kitchen, and then taking them up the small wooden staircase from there to the servants' quarters, high up in the tower wing, rather than going past Margaret's bedroom into the new wing passage, and risking meeting her along there. Their new room had no double bed, but two small ones were soon pushed together. Madeleine liked the room because it looked out over the back and one side of the house, rather than just the front, as her old one had done. She bustled around arranging and packing away her things. There was a small wooden chest, and she gave that space to Ryan for him to keep his meagre possessions in.

Later in the evening, Madeleine was bemused and puzzled as to why she was allowed to be alone in the bedroom with Ryan, after all her parents had said. She was mystified that they had made no move to stop her from taking him to her bed. A happy thought occurred to her, "They've not stopped us being alone here. Perhaps they're coming to understand after all."

"I wish it were so. We married in secret, and they'll never forgive me for it. I took you from their house and brought you back tied to me forever. They may be allowing us this time because they think we've already slept together...but I think there's another reason..." Ryan paused, "...remember what Nancy and Sarah joked with you about?"

"Yes..."

"You know nothing of the joining of a man and a woman?"

"No...but I..." Now she was shy and concerned. Did this admission mean she wouldn't be satisfactory to him as a wife?

"Your mother...stepmother...believes me to be a boorish oaf. She's made that plain. She believes that I'll hurt you. She thinks you'll run screaming to her to save you after a few hours in my company, having been badly used by me."

"You'd never hurt me."

"The first moment between a man and a woman, always brings a brief sting as the woman is 'opened' to the man, but with gentleness, that's all, just a brief moment. I'll prove it to you."

Madeleine knew that despite Ryan's young age, she wasn't his first bed mate by far. She knew that several of the serving maids at nearby estates were furious and eaten up with jealously that Ryan had abandoned their beds for her. She didn't mind that he was considered adept, because it meant that he didn't rush at her like a raging bull, as she'd heard tell other men did. Older women, already married, had warned her of such men, although she hadn't always understood their warnings. Some of the women had told her that they'd been shy of their marriage bed ever since the first night. But when Ryan took Madeleine it was different...

She was scared and happy at the same time. She had no experience of men and had no idea of what was to happen between her and Ryan, only that a physical act would be expected of her. He came closer, until their bodies touched, pressed, fitted, and she trembled. He put both his hands in her hair and kissed her on the mouth. When she'd gone to him in the barn she'd thought she was quite ready for this, so it was strange that she was a little afraid now, but as his hands slid down and caressed her neck, she shivered. Maybe the older women, with their talk of being hurt by men, had affected her after all. But Ryan had told her that he wouldn't hurt her, and she trusted him.

He seemed to read her thoughts, because he said, "Don't be afraid, I'll never hurt you, never. We have all night." He kissed her again, this time harder, his hands cupping her head. His lips pressed more firmly on hers, his tongue seeking entry into her mouth, and suddenly she answered his hunger with her own. Her arms rose unbidden, and circled his waist. She could feel a part of him, low down, pushing against the confines of his breeches, and she understood that men were very different from women. Then she felt an answering surge of heat rush through her own body, and she moaned softly at the feeling, opening her mouth to him. He pushed fiercely against her body, and she trembled again, knowing that this time it was really going to happen, whatever it was. This time there'd be no turning back.

Ryan undressed her slowly, caressing and kissing every tiny part of her as it was exposed. He kissed her in unexpected places; the inside of her elbow joint on the soft skin creases there, the underside of her wrist, her ears, the bottoms of her feet, and a little later the insides of her thighs. It was all very mysterious, but reality gradually faded away, and her whole being centred on the pleasure that was growing in parts of her body she'd barely been aware of before. She couldn't have stopped even if she'd wanted to.

When she finally stood naked before him, and saw his eyes turn intense as he gazed at her, she was filled with an unexpected sense of power over him. His expression showed a devotion to her, and a need for her, that she'd never seen in anyone before. He caressed her in places she had never been touched, or touched herself in before, gently restraining her shyness, and encouraging her to relax and trust him. After moments she experienced an ecstasy she had never though possible. Wave after wave of intense pleasure left her gasping with delight.

When he took off his own clothes, her first sight of a naked man was both wonderful and terrifying. When he laid over her, she finally understood how a man and a woman were meant to unite and she felt a moment of fear. She gasped and clutched at his shoulders. Then he looked down into her eyes, and quite deliberately, he smiled at her. She found herself smiling back. He held her gaze while he joined with her, his gentle smile never faltering, and that contact calmed her. This strange being was still her beloved Ryan after all. She felt no more fear. The small stab of pain when it came was exquisite in that she knew it meant they were finally, really, as one. It passed in a fleeting second, and from then, all was pleasure.

When Ryan was spent, he cradled Madeleine in his arms and she felt precious and safe in the heat from the fire, and she drifted into a relaxed sleep. She woke up some hours later, in the early morning light. It was raining heavily outside, and the sound of it lashing against the window was strangely pleasing as they snuggled together. She reached for *him* this time, and over the next hours he taught her so much about his own body, and hers.

She had two vivid memories of their first joining. When Ryan first gazed upon her naked body, his eyes and his respectful manner gave her a feeling of great sway over him. To feel such power over one so strong wasn't something she'd ever expected. The other surprise was the pleasure he gave to her. No woman had ever spoken to her of the pleasure a man could give a woman, if he was considerate enough. When she awoke to his presence in the early hours, she felt nothing but welcome for his attentions. Nothing was more joyous to her than having his hands touch her. Despite the heavy rain pounding against the windows, she felt so secure and warm in the comfort of his arms. After that night the love she felt for him reached new dimensions. To have a man such as this, she thought, was surely every woman's desire.

CHAPTER ELEVEN

It was surely no coincidence that the very next day, Mr Pennington came to call. Madeleine had known that her stepmother had planned to give her to him in marriage, but she'd done nothing to encourage her stepmother to believe that she would agree to it. Pennington was fifty years old, older than Margaret herself, and thirty-four years Madeleine's senior. He was of no interest to her and never had been. Margaret knew it but it was obvious that she had refused to accept it. He was a rich and influential man, and all she could see were the benefits to her name, and the additional power it would bring her if he became attached to the family.

As the carriage drew up outside, Margaret left a servant to greet him, ran upstairs to Madeleine's new bedchamber and was pleased to find Madeleine alone there. She was sure that Madeleine would be ready by then to 'see sense', and rushed in with rash words.

"Come child," she said, dragging Madeleine by the arm, "We may yet save you from yourself. This ridiculous marriage can be annulled. By now I'm sure you've realised your mistake?" She glanced meaningfully at the bed, raising her eyebrows questioningly. "Mr Pennington need never know if we act quickly." She smiled, so sure that Madeleine would be pleased to obey her, having spent a night in the company of the Irish peasant.

"No!" Madeleine protested.

"No? You must see sense! You must know that you've made a mistake!"

"*No.*"

"Oh my God, you can't still be besotted! You must be mad! Do you know what a fortune Pennington is worth?"

"I don't need his fortune…" Madeleine responded, "…and I most certainly don't need him, or any other man," and she too glanced meaningfully at the bed, as a small and satisfied smile curled her mouth. This gesture was unwise, inflaming Margaret still further as she grasped the meaning behind it.

"Harlot!" she shrieked. "Filthy little bitch! He's already ruined you!"

Before Madeleine could answer, Margaret glanced out of the window to see what the situation was below. Madeleine looked over Margaret's shoulder saw that Ryan was down there. He was standing with one foot planted firmly on the step of Mr Pennington's carriage step, thereby stopping him getting down from the carriage. Mr Pennington was blustering, standing up, hands flapping, and it was obvious from the expression on his face that he was threatening Ryan in some way. Margaret took in the scene that was playing out below, and left the room in a horrified hurry.

Madeleine kept watching from the window, and she saw Ryan lean forward and take hold of Mr Pennington by his collar. He said something, and Mr Pennington went very still, and then subsided back into his seat with a boneless fluidity. Ryan let go of him and signalled to the driver to move off. At this point Margaret appeared on the steps, and at the sight of her Mr Pennington hurriedly instructed his driver to whip the horses on. The carriage left the grounds almost at the gallop, throwing up gravel, dust streaming out behind it. Margaret started to shout at Ryan, and Madeleine saw him quickly turn on his heel and return inside, ignoring her.

When Ryan came back up to Madeleine, she asked him what had

been said. He told her that Mr Pennington had been demanding to see her, refusing to believe she was married and calling Ryan a liar. Ryan had asked Mr Pennington if he should take this to be a challenge to a duel, and that was what had caused the gentleman's hasty departure.

Two days after Mr Pennington called at the house, Ryan waited for Margaret in the passage from the dairy. He was pretty sure it was going to be a waste of time trying to talk to her, but he felt he had to try. If only he could convince her, then life could be happy and long, instead of always having to live under the dark cloud of his future fate. Margaret always visited the dairy at that time of day and he was waiting for her to come back, knowing that they would most likely have some privacy there. He stood concealed in the shadows of the barn steps, only stepping out into the light as she walked along the brick-lined passage. She stopped and took a step back, startled by his sudden appearance.

"What do you want?" she snapped.

Ryan raised his hands in a placating gesture, not wanting her to feel threatened, and answered her quietly, "Just a moment to speak with you."

She didn't answer him and folded her arms, impatience written across her face, so he carried on, "I know very well that I am not what you hoped for."

"In no conceivable way!" she interrupted, glaring at him.

"I know, I know," he carried on. "You've made that very obvious, but the fact is we are married. I'm not here to try to gain anything from you or Madeleine's father. I really do love Madeleine and I am hoping that you will allow that to count for something."

"Love won't pay taxes! Love won't feed you! Oh, why did you

come here? She had every chance of a future, and now you've ruined everything for her!"

Ryan dropped his hands to his sides. He surrendered his eye contact with Margaret and stared down at the ground. He paused, gathering his thoughts, one boot stirring the dust underfoot. Margaret pursed her lips, and her pinched nose showed her impatience.

He spoke again quietly, he hoped persuasively, his eyes still downcast, encouraging her to feel in charge, as that seemed to be the only thing that ever pleased her. "I can't change who or what I am, and I can't stop loving Madeleine. But it's done. We're married now and it would make things so much better for all of us if you could only accept it. Please, tell me what you want of me, save leaving without her, and I will try to satisfy you and Edwin."

Margaret's eyes flashed angrily, and her voice lashed at him, "Nothing you could do would save you from my wrath! Only death would save you! Now get out of my path and take care never to stand in my way again lest I'm tempted to send you into the embrace of death myself!"

She started to push past him but he stepped sideways, barring her way. "Very well," he said, as he lifted his eyes to hers once more. "Treat me however you see fit. But I warn you, never harm my wife, for that would be a mistake. I have a temper too, and it wouldn't be controlled if Madeleine were hurt in any way." His met her eyes fully, his own glinting with dangerous possibilities that she must have seen. He felt her anger turn to fear for a moment as he stepped aside, and she hurriedly went past him.

However, Margaret must not have believed him because she next turned her bullying tactics on Madeleine. It was very common in those days, and quite accepted, for parents to thrash their unruly offspring, even the girls. It was usually done with a stiff cane, which bruised but did not cut. They tried this only the once on Madeleine, in an attempt to make her renounce her love for Ryan. As a result, Ryan terrified Margaret so much that she never dared to try it again. It also made her fear him as much as she already hated him.

Madeleine was unexpectedly called to the drawing room. It was quite late into the evening, but Ryan was still out in the fields because of the urgent need to gather in the hay harvest. Margaret and Edwin were both present in the room, the woman looking smug. Edwin on the other hand, was shame-faced and would not look at his daughter. Two of the rougher type of the farm's casual labourers stood behind Margaret. They only worked on the farm during harvesting, and Madeleine was very puzzled as to what they were doing in the house.

It became all too clear as Margaret spoke, "Madeleine, your father and I have discussed things, and we both agree that you have become totally wayward and out of hand. You show us no respect. You have had no discipline in years, and that's why we find ourselves in this predicament. You need to be brought to heel. We have been very patient with you, allowing you more than enough time to learn from your mistakes, but now you must be taught obedience once and for all. Your marriage to this Irish peasant will be annulled immediately. Do you understand?"

Madeleine sighed tiredly, not this again. "No," she said wearily, "When will you both understand? Our vows were made and meant for life. No-one will part us."

"You will learn differently," Margaret continued. "When I was a child any disobedience was curbed as yours will be curbed now. You have been getting away with your hard-headedness for quite long enough."

Margaret signalled to the two men and at the same she time produced a long thick cane from behind her back, and Madeleine realised what her stepmother meant to do. The two men moved towards Madeleine and stopped her as she tried to escape through the door.

The girl ran to her father in desperation and grasped his hands, pleading: "Father, you can't allow this thing! Please! Father!" but he would not look at her. Instead he turned away.

"It is no use, child," Margaret said, wicked smile on her face. "Your father has taken my advice in this matter." At this the two men took hold of Madeleine's arms and propelled her across the room to the big oak table. They pushed her face down against the polished surface. She was very afraid, and could see her own rapid breaths forming a pool of mist on the shiny wood an inch from her eyes. Margaret smacked the cane against her skirts as she approached her step-daughter.

In the meantime, Ryan, who had been in the hay meadows, two fields away from the house, suddenly stopped working to stare at the incredible sight of Nancy's stout figure rushing towards him as fast as she was able. He ran to meet her. Gossip in the servants' quarters had alerted Nancy to Margaret's wicked scheme. The cook was puffing so heavily that Ryan thought she would collapse, but between gasps, she managed to tell him enough so that he set off for the house at a dead run.

The first thing Madeleine knew of Ryan's arrival was when the door to the dining room suddenly flew open with such force that it banged into the wall behind it. At that moment Margaret was standing over her stepdaughter, the cane raised in her clenched fist, ready to strike the first blow. That blow never landed on its intended target, because at the noise from the door she immediately turned the stick on Ryan. But his charge was so fast that he was upon her before she could hit out. She let out a startled shriek as he snatched the cane from her hand and snapped it in two across his thigh, with a loud crack.

Margaret ran to Edwin, who looked terrified. Ryan advanced on the two men who held Madeleine. The ferocity of his expression was such that the men, who had been told that they must merely keep hold of young woman, immediately let go of her. Raising their hands to Ryan in a placating gesture, they dodged around him and made off through the door. Ryan took Madeleine in his arms and held her close. Madeleine looked up at his face, clinging to him just as tightly.

"Are you all right?" he asked, anxiously.

"Yes, she didn't touch me."

"As well she did not!" Ryan turned to face Margaret, so angry that his words spat at her like snake venom: "This time you should heed my warning! If you ever lay a hand on her again…" he paused, his eyes narrowing, "…I will kill you! You may escape justice for your treatment of others…" he let go of Madeleine and stepped up close to Margaret. She drew back involuntarily at the naked rage in his eyes as he continued in a low and threatening voice, "…but if you ever touch Madeleine again, do not doubt me, you will *die*."

"Edwin!" she screamed. "Do something in my defence!" But he was obviously too afraid for his frail bones, and he did not move.

"Perhaps he at least feels some of the shame that you should feel," Ryan continued, his blazing eyes inches from Margaret's. He raised a clenched fist above her, as if he was going to hit her. He held it close to her face so that she went pale. "This time," he said, "I have arrived in time to save you from yourself, but don't ignore this warning a second time."

Even by the time they had reached their bedchamber, Ryan was still upset. He paced the room, unable to calm down. Madeleine started to undress in the hope of distracting him, pirouetting around as she discarded her dress and then her petticoat. This ruse worked, and soon he cradled her in his arms, stroking the bare skin of her back.

"She should thank God that she did not mark you," he said, his eyes dark.

CHAPTER TWELVE

Madeleine discovered as time went by that Ryan was a man of sharp contrasts. If she were threatened, he appeared fearless, even arrogant sometimes, with a short, dark, Irish temper. The same applied if someone else weaker than him was in trouble. When it came to defending himself though, he was not so confident or well-equipped. For some weeks he and Madeleine had managed to keep a low profile, and Margaret seemed to have backed off because Ryan had intimidated her. Eventually though, her obsession returned, and she finally found a way to break through his armour to his weak spot.

Having obviously come up with a cunning ploy, she made an unexpected visit to the kitchen while Ryan and Madeleine were sitting at the big oak table eating their supper. She stalked around the big room, running a critical hand over the pots and pans that hung from hooks in the ceiling, tut tutting over any speck of dirt that she found, real or imagined. She picked up a poker and prodded the fire irritably. Logs dropped, broke up, snapping and flaring into flame, imitating her mood, as she jabbed at them. After a circuit of the room, she stopped at the table, opposite Ryan. He sighed resignedly, obviously recognising the signs of trouble. The truce was over and he was to be her target for the day. Margaret reached across the table and pulled Ryan's half-full plate of food away from him. He knew better than to rise to her bait, so he merely stared back at her neutrally, showing no emotion.

"I see that we're still feeding you more than you're worth," she sneered.

He didn't answer. With luck, he hoped, she would soon tire of her game, and leave to seek out easier prey. She pushed the plate back angrily, so that the food slopped onto the table. Ryan resumed eating, but Madeleine didn't, her face a stony mask of fury, as she shoved her own plate away, all appetite gone.

Margaret pounced on her instantly. "Madeleine, don't waste good food, especially when it's good food this good-for-nothing hasn't earned!"

Madeleine didn't have Ryan's forbearance, or his patience, and she snapped back, "My husband works very hard for you, harder than the other workers, who are paid more than him, and you know that's the truth."

Ryan nudged Madeleine, nodded his head towards the back door, and got to his feet, stretching and yawning as if leaving had been his intention all along. He hoped she would follow his lead. A confrontation was not desirable. He walked to the back door, and thankfully Madeleine got up and followed him outside. Ryan was well-aware of Margaret's feelings towards him; he was a 'non-person' as far as she was concerned. This was confirmed by something he'd noticed. Margaret had never, ever, addressed him by name. He never heard her say it. He led Madeleine to a stone seat in the rose garden, a small private place off the kitchen garden, and they sat down. No sooner had they done so though than Margaret followed them into the garden.

Marching up to where the couple sat she sneered, "There's still much work to do in the fields. I would have thought you'd have been ashamed to sit idly while others work. Have you no pride?"

"Ryan's been working since five o' clock this morning!" Madeleine reminded her.

But she was unstoppable, "What kind of weakling are you?" she asked him. This comment sounded totally ridiculous as Ryan stood up, towering over her as he did by a good eleven inches. He was ready to leave her presence again, rather than get into an argument, but she stood in his path so that he couldn't easily pass. Ryan stared down at her. He had two choices, either to push past her or to sit down again, but he decided to do neither. He was heartily sick of this cat and mouse game, and for once lost his temper in his own defence. He quickly put his hands on either side of Margaret's waist and lifted her bodily out of the way, putting her back down at the side of the pathway, then he and Madeleine both hurried past her.

Livid, Margaret pushed roughly back past them both from behind, knocking Madeleine into the rose bed and stumbling into it herself as she pushed past Ryan. She nimbly regained her feet and turned in front of him to block his path again.

"Don't ever dare to touch me!" she screamed, white with rage and indignation. She continued vengefully, "What kind of upbringing did you have that it allows you to behave so impudently? Your own mother and father must have been glad to be rid of you!" She must have immediately seen, though he tried to hide it from her, that her remarks had hit a sensitive nerve, because she smiled mercilessly.

Ryan couldn't help it. His face flinched and his eyes filled at the mention of his mother. His grief was too new, too raw, and too personal to hide. He knew that Margaret had finally found a way to get through his defences.

Margaret's brown eyes grew sly, "If you even had a father! The Irish slut that spat you out probably never even knew who your father was!" Ryan winced, as if someone had hit him. He went very still, his jaw line rigid. He stared at her for several long seconds, his eyes deep and dark. There was a grain of truth in what the woman had said, in that his mother had children by two men, but this English bitch had no right to talk about her that way. His mother had been an angel compared to her.

Finally, cutting each word off tightly he said, "My mother may not have enjoyed the wealth you have, but she had that which you secretly long for, and yet will *never* be able to buy, she was *loved*! No-one will *ever* love you!"

Margaret stepped back in alarm as he put up one arm to push her aside, and he brushed past her. Without a backward glance he left the gardens at a fast walk, and headed towards the woods. Madeleine glared at Margaret for a long silent beat, and then she hurried after Ryan.

She found him leaning against the big oak tree. He had his back to her and had his hands bracing him against the trunk, both arms rigid and his head down. When she reached him she put her hands tentatively on his shoulders and could feel what she presumed was a deep anger quivering in him. He turned to his wife in a rush, and gathered her into his arms before she could even register his expression. He held her tight and she gradually realised that he was still trembling, but not with anger - he was crying.

After a while Ryan stood up again, his grief purged for a while. His blue eyes still sparkled with the tears. Madeleine thought that maybe at last he would be ready to tell her about his mother, as he never had before. The loss of her seemed like an open wound, and in the past talking about it had only appeared to make the pain worse. Madeleine waited to see if this was the time. He leaned back against the tree, slid down the trunk, and sat at the base, drawing his wife down to sit between his legs. She leaned back against him, the back of her head resting on his chest. He put his arms around her and she took his hands in hers, wrapping him around her like a cloak.

"Do you want to tell me about your mother?" she asked gently. "I know so little of your past."

He didn't answer for a few moments. Then he took off his wedding ring, stared at it for a moment or two, and held it up to the light so that he could see the inscription that was written inside. Then he said, almost in a whisper, "If you want me to," he swallowed.

"Please," she coaxed.

"I'm not who you think I am."

Madeleine didn't know what to say to that. Whatever could he mean? She hesitated, and then answered, "It doesn't matter. I still love you…whoever you are. Just tell me."

It seemed to be easier for him to tell her with her sitting in front of him the way she was, probably so that he didn't have to look at her face while he spoke. While he told her his story he turned the gold Fitzgerald ring round and around in his fingers. Hesitantly, he related his true history to Madeleine.

In the middle of the telling, she leapt to her feet and turned and stared at him in amazement. "But, that means…it means that you are an aristocrat, of noble blood! You are higher born than *her!* She has no blue blood in her. If she knew then she'd *have* to change her feelings for you. It would give her the noble marriage for me that she wanted…I…" Madeleine's excited voice petered out as she realised that Ryan was shaking his head at her.

"I've had this conversation with Nancy. It wouldn't have the effect either of you hope for. It wouldn't take her long to discover my illegitimacy, even though I have the Fitzgerald ring. The label of 'bastard' would just be one more thing for her to throw at me...besides, if the Fitzgerald's got wind of where I am...anything could happen."

"Oh," Madeleine sat back down at his feet, deflated. "You told Nancy?"

"Yes, I only didn't tell you because...because, everything happened so fast, and it would have made things so complicated. I've been denying that part of my life. I only told Nancy because when I first came here she was the only one I could really talk to. I didn't mean to hurt you."

She couldn't be angry with him, besides, his talk of 'anything happening' had scared her. "It's all right. I just wish that your birth could be used to help us." She subsided into his arms. She decided to be brave, but then just as quickly, knew she couldn't be, and looking anxiously up at his face she asked, "What did you mean by 'anything could happen'?"

"If they knew where I was, which they don't, they might...only might, come after me. My half-brother would rather I didn't exist."

"Oh, God!"

"Like I said, they have no idea where I am, and so long as your stepmother doesn't know about my past, we have nothing to worry about. Besides, I have changed so much, since being with you that they probably wouldn't know me anyway. Here, I'm free. With you, I'm free. Whatever happens I don't want you to forget that."

"Whatever happens? Now you're scaring me again."

"I didn't mean to, I just meant whatever anyone ever says, whatever you might come to think, it was my choice to stay here, and in staying here I *also* made a choice to be *free*."

"I know," Madeleine said quietly, "that I'm not the only one who has given up things in this relationship. You gave up your traveling ways to be with me. Sometimes that makes me afraid..."

"Afraid? Of what?"

"That I am holding you back, keeping you still, when you'd rather be moving."

"No, not any more..."

"I just want you to know that I *do* understand, and that I will try and be whatever you need, right here in this place."

"You *are* all that I need. You are my sky, my sun, my moon. You're the very wind in my hair. I don't need to move anymore to feel the wind." He took her hands in his and brought them up to his mouth, kissing them. Then he continued his story to the end, only missing out his dalliance with Glenda. The ending of the story delighted her, because he said simply, "And that day, at first sight, I fell in love with you, and I'm *still* falling," which made her smile, and turn her face up to be kissed.

CHAPTER THIRTEEN

The bringing in of a successful harvest was always celebrated with a market and fair. In 1612, the King had decreed that Hambledon qualified for this honour, thereby also bestowing on it the title of 'town', rather than village. Ryan and Madeleine were able to attend in 1638, for the first time since they had become husband and wife. Madeleine was very excited, and keen to show off her new husband to the townsfolk. She followed Ryan around the estate all morning, trying to help him hurry through his chores, but mostly getting in the way like an over-exuberant puppy. Finally they were ready and set off, with a hamper of food and drink put together by Nancy.

The whole populace had gathered on the banks of the pond with picnic baskets in abundance, and Ryan and Madeleine sat down together to eat their food in the long, dry grass. When they'd finished, they packed up their spent feast and started to walk through the market. Underfoot, because of the shortage of rain, the street was inches deep in soft dust, which coated their shoes and the hem of Madeleine's dress with fine, gritty powder. However, the normally drab town was bedecked with streamers, flags, and banners, and there was so much to see, so many wonderful things for sale. There were reams of woollen cloth, hung game birds, rabbits and hares, and even the occasional half-hog. There were rainbows of ribbons, heaps of pots and pans, cheeses, horse-bells and jugs of ale. Some of the stallholders were village people selling their wares but others, such as the itinerant knife-grinder and the tinker with his tin goods, made their living travelling around the countryside, with all their trappings in tow.

Madeleine was drawn to the colourful ribbons, and after a while Ryan grew silent beside her. Looking at him she could easily read his thoughts. He knew that this was the first year of her life when she hadn't gone to the fair with her parents, first Rebecca and Edwin and then Margaret and Edwin. He must have also known that on previous visits she would have been bought pretty things, whereas he of course could not buy her anything. To him, the pretty ribbons probably symbolised everything Madeleine had given up to be his wife.

She laughed softly and dismissed the ribbons and cloths with a gesture of her hand, "Childish!"

Ryan smiled. He must have known that this was contrived, but would have appreciated her intentions.

They carried on walking, and their steps took them past the knife-grinder. Madeleine found herself shuddering at the sight of the small, weasel-like man, dirty as he was, and almost toothless. His face was creased and rough, and she felt an unaccountable uneasiness as he looked back at her. As they moved further on, she saw the same face peering out at her from behind the ale stall, as if he had darted ahead to be there in front of them. She let go of Ryan's hand and slid her arm more securely though his, drawing them into a closer contact. She felt safer immediately, although she couldn't help but glance back again, and sure enough the man's eyes were still fastened on her like leeches. She snuggled yet closer to Ryan's comforting presence, and he too looked back to see the reason for her unease. As he saw the man she was looking at, he seemed to share some of her concern, because she felt his arm muscles tightened protectively under her hand.

They strolled on towards the fair, where the men of the town fought to be declared stronger, faster, and better than each other. The bare-knuckled fist fighting was brutal. Fists smacked into faces with meaty slaps. The men and women in the crowd reflected its brutality, baying for blood as they watched the contestants lose teeth, and cut each others' faces as they fought. On the far side of the meadow there was a horse race in progress, and Ryan and Madeleine stood and watched it for a while. The animals taking part were many and varied. They ranged from tiny hairy ponies, ridden without saddles, by small wiry boys who clung to their backs like limpets, to giant dray horses with massive feet that pounded past the ponies as if they could have trampled over them without even noticing them.

Various feats of pure strength were taking place and Madeleine grasped Ryan's arm excitedly. "Surely," she pleaded, "you must take part?" He was surprisingly reluctant, not seeming to relish the attention of the townsfolk. He resisted her attempts at persuading him to join in the single-handed tug o' war that took place over the stream, the loser being pulled into the water. Finally, after much encouragement from Madeleine, determined as she was to show him off, he agreed to become a contestant in the water-wagon pulling competition. Each man was harnessed to a heavy wooden cart and he had to pull it along. If they were equally matched then barrels of water would be added to the weight one by one, until one of the men couldn't move it any longer, and the other would be declared the winner. It was a gruelling task, and most of the men preferred to just watch and bet on the outcome, rather than take part themselves, so there were only four takers for the prize of a whole hog.

Madeleine was proud of her husband's strength as he threw his shoulder into the harness and the cart followed him over the ten yard line. In the first round he won easily, and the final would be a head-to-head pull between him and the other winner. They were to drag a cart each, side by side, and the winner would be the one who towed his cart furthest across the rough grass.

Both men were given a short rest, so Ryan dropped to the grass beside Madeleine where she sat. He laid on his back, stretched out, his arms crossed over his face to shield his eyes from the bright sun. She could see that his shirt was damp in places with sweat and that it clung to him. The hair on his brow was wet with it and it was curled into glossy tendrils. Beads of moisture rolled down his face, falling onto the bone-dry ground where it was greedily sucked up by the thirsty earth. Madeleine took the water flask from the picnic basket, and offered it to him. He took a few sips and then upended the remainder over his head.

After a few minutes, the two men were called to their task. Ryan's rival was Thomas Hendry, a beefy man, weighing much more than Ryan did. Thomas was red in complexion and had a large beer belly that hung over his belt. As they were fastened into their harnesses Thomas tried to taunt Ryan into rashness.

"Irish *boy,* you don't have a chance. I'm the local champion at this. You'll drop dead going up against me! You're going to make a fool of yourself!"

As the starter dropped his flag, Ryan and Thomas leaned into their harnesses. Thomas threw his whole weight into his and his wagon jolted into forward movement, picking up a rolling speed, as every vein and sinew stood out over his face, neck and arms. He certainly made a powerful picture. Ryan however took up a much steadier pull, his wagon moving much more gradually and smoothly. Thomas heaved, throwing himself constantly against the straps, striving for greater and greater speed. Soon he was twenty paces ahead of Ryan, who in contrast to Thomas, moved with a steady rhythm, pacing relentlessly forward. People started cheering Thomas as he forged ahead, seeing an obvious winner, and that their betting money was safe. But just like in the story of the tortoise and the hare, things were not as simple as they seemed.

Thomas was expending his energy in a display of manliness, whilst Ryan was using his intelligence and conserving his strength wisely. Thomas pulled his wagon quickly, in jerks and starts to the fifty yard mark, and then, looking totally arrogant and sure that he had done enough, he dropped to the ground between the shafts, to the praise of his neighbours. They gathered around him in congratulation, money starting to pass to the winning gamblers. Then, quite suddenly, people started shouting, and they all realised that Ryan was still coming, and catching up fast. They urged Thomas to his feet, especially those that had placed their wager on him, as Ryan's cart was now only twenty paces behind. Thomas staggered to his feet, reeling breathlessly, and he tried to re-start his cart, but he couldn't do it. He looked as if his muscles had turned as feeble as water.

He struggled futilely as the other cart overtook him, and then had no choice but to admit defeat as Ryan pulled it another twenty paces. Madeleine rushed forward and threw her arms around her husband. He was breathing heavily and smelled of musky sweat. She found the natural scent of him very appealing, and breathed it in. Ryan's prize was handed to him, and it was a *live,* squealing, half-grown hoglet. The two of them had to head for home then, because the hoglet was an unwilling captive, and thrashed relentlessly in Ryan's arms. In the middle of the woodland, they took pity on their prize and let it go. The pig ran, grunting and squealing, into the undergrowth, and quickly disappeared.

A few days later Madeleine discovered why the knife-grinder had given her such a feeling of foreboding. It was a beautiful day and Ryan was working on the far side of the woods, and although the trees formed a dark and lonely country, she decided to walk and meet him, to surprise him. As she went further into the woods, the thick canopy cut of almost all of the sunlight, and the only sounds were her footsteps, as she followed the track that had been made by countless carts as they toiled to and fro, and birdsong. It was so peaceful and tranquil that she decided to take a short cut through the narrower trails made by badger and deer. Cobwebs festooned the low branches and bushes and as she brushed past, they showered her with refreshing water droplets that had been trapped in them. The hem of her dress wafted across the grass stems under her feet. Fern fronds grew across the path at head height and she had to stoop and push them aside. They closed behind her like a living curtain. It was peaceful and secret.

Suddenly Madeleine stopped, listening keenly, her head tilted to one side. The birds had all suddenly fallen silent and she could hear rustling behind her. A deer? Wild boar? She hoped not, as boar could be very aggressive. She thought it best to hurry on, just in case. A few paces further and she stopped again, listening anxiously. This time there was a sharp snap as something trod heavily on a fallen twig. Not a deer then, which would have moved more stealthily. The rustling continued after she had stopped moving, and her blood froze. Intuitively she suddenly knew that she was being stalked, and there was only one creature in those woods that would stalk a human – another human. She looked back over her shoulder, but she couldn't see anything through the thick greenery, and she wished she hadn't left the main path. The beautiful living curtain that had closed behind her was no longer serene, but full of danger.

The footsteps behind her grew louder as if the person had grown bolder, and Madeleine knew she was in real trouble. If this person had friendly intentions they would have made themselves known, not stayed hidden from her. She didn't know what to do. Call for Ryan, who would be within earshot very soon, or stay silent so that her possible attacker wouldn't know she had heard him? She felt hunted, as terror-stricken as any rabbit with a fox close behind it. The trees ahead were just starting to thin, and she decided to yell to Ryan. She opened her mouth to scream, but it was cut off as she was grabbed from behind by her hair. She was pulled over backwards onto her back, her wind, and the scream, cut off suddenly.

The man, revealed at last, quickly shoved a dirty hand over her mouth and threw himself bodily on top of her. It was the knife-grinder from the fair. He let go of her hair and his free hand started to pull her gown up. She tried to hit him, but her blows were weak with fear and made no impact on him. He grunted with satisfaction as his hand found the skin of her bare leg, and his fingernails scrambled up it like the legs of a terrible, clawed spider. He muttered, and his breathing grew faster with need, as his hand rifled through her petticoats. As his hand briefly touched her where no-one but her husband should have done, and she recoiled, he gasped and hissed.

He let go of her mouth, to free both his hands, and at that moment she heard a distant shout, "Madeleine?"

She never knew whether Ryan had heard the scuffle from where he was, or if some link through their souls had told him she was there and in danger, but the sound of his voice gave her strength. She heaved herself upwards under the man, and her right hand became a talon, clenched and clawed. She tore at his forehead, drawing blood. The man glanced down at her face through a red veil that drizzled over his eyes, and then looked worriedly towards the direction of Ryan's voice. Obviously realising that the tables were turning, the man let go of Madeleine, scrambled up, and ran away, disappearing quickly into the surrounding trees.

Ryan appeared, running, through the thinning woodland. He rushed to Madeleine and helped her to her feet. He scanned around, his expression furious as he guessed what might have been taking place. He was looking for her assailant, but the man had vanished. At the sight of Ryan, Madeleine had almost collapsed with relief. He drew her into the safe circle of his arms, still looking around fiercely for the danger.

"What happened?" he asked.

She replied, her mouth close to his ear as he held her, "It was the knife-grinder from the fair, he…he…" she hesitated; fearing Ryan's reaction, which she knew would be ferocious. If she said too much too quickly, Ryan would chase the man down and probably kill him, and she had no desire for a murder to darken her love's soul. "I'm not harmed," she reassured him, "just shaken."

"What did he do?" Ryan demanded.

"He came upon me from behind, forced me to the ground…"

It was enough. Ryan went rigid with fury. "Which direction did he take?" he asked in a voice that was as hard as iron and yet as brittle as glass.

"I don't know, perhaps towards the village. But…Ryan…"

He looked at her. She could see that he was torn between a need to pursue and run down the evil villain, and the need to stay with her and be her protector.

"Please. Don't leave me. Let God see that he's punished. I'm still afraid and I need you to hold me." Madeleine could feel the coiled springs of tension beneath his shirt. "He might come back if you leave me. I can't be sure which path he took. He might still be nearby, waiting for you to leave. Please, please just take me home."

Reluctantly he agreed, and with his arm tight about her, they set off. Madeleine felt grubby, and she could still feel a tingle in all the places where the despicable man had touched her. She smothered her shudders, not wanting to encourage Ryan to chase after her attacker. She thought that it was very unlikely that the knife-grinder would ever dare to show his face in the town again, and at least now she was safe, and had felt so from the first touch of Ryan's hand.

CHAPTER FOUREEN

In the winter of that year an epidemic of flu struck the estate. It was mostly the farm workers who caught it, and some of them died because they didn't have warm places to rest in or anyone to look after them. Most of the upper classes were spared because of the silver they regularly ingested from their drinking cups. They were protected, albeit unknowingly by its natural antibiotic qualities. It wasn't surprising that Ryan caught it because he mixed with the outside workers as no-one else in the house did.

Madeleine knew something was wrong with him as soon as she woke up, because it was already past dawn, the sky outside the window was slashed with pink and amber, and yet he was still asleep beside her. Normally he would have left the house to go and work by 5am, while it was still dark. He seemed to be deeply asleep. Madeleine touched his face gently to wake him up, and when he didn't respond right away, she rubbed his shoulder. His skin was as hot as fiery coals. He woke up and said he was very thirsty so she fetched him some flat ale.

Despite her protests, Ryan insisted on getting dressed and going out to the dairy, promising that he would come back if he felt worse. She had felt his breath, hot on her face as he had spoken, and his shirt had already been clammy with sweat, but she'd had no choice but to let him go. He as always had been concerned at what her parents would think of him if he didn't show up for work.

Madeleine had said that she didn't care what they thought. She'd pointed out the frond-like patterns of frost on the insides of the windows, despite the fire burning in the grate, and told him it was too cold for him to go outside with a fever, but he wouldn't listen.

So, despite her concern, Madeleine found herself watching with misgivings from the back window as Ryan crossed the yard and passed by the barn, on his way to the dairy. His shoulders sagged, and he gave a cough as he breathed in the frigid air. The bitter cold was so intense that clouds of white vapour appeared as he breathed out. Then he disappeared from sight, and Madeleine decided to go down to the kitchen. Nancy was bustling around, trying to do ten jobs at once, and she told Madeleine that she hadn't been able to persuade Ryan to eat anything before he left.

Madeleine prepared him some hot broth, which she planned to take out to him. But when she went to the dairy with it, Ryan wasn't there. They told her that a cow had fallen into a ditch and become trapped. It was bogged down and in danger of drowning in the mud if no-one saved it. The only two men available had been Ryan and one other, so they had gone with ropes to pull the cow out of the mud.

Madeleine went back indoors and was watching anxiously from the kitchen window when they finally came back. Ryan was staggering, and the other man had to help him across the yard. Madeleine ran out in a panic and almost slipped on the treacherous, icy surface of the flagstones. She helped the other workman get Ryan upstairs, so difficult in the narrow back staircase. Eventually though, they managed to get him to the top and into the bedroom, where he collapsed onto the bed. His clothes were sodden and his skin was freezing, racking him with uncontrollable shivers. As the workman hurriedly left the room, he cast a backward glance at the bed, and crossed himself. This meant two things. First, the man was thanking the Lord that he'd been spared the sickness so far, and second, he believed Ryan would die. Madeleine shuddered. She would never allow it. She couldn't bear it.

There was no-one who she could call on for help, because those who weren't already stricken themselves were exhausted from nursing those who were. Ryan's cheeks were flushed, and although he still shivered violently, his skin had turned hot through the wet clothes. Madeleine quickly began to pull them off. It was difficult, for Ryan was curled up tightly, trying to get warm. But eventually she threw the last soaked item onto the soggy heap on the floor. She drew the blankets up around him, and then she climbed into the bed and wrapped her body around his, to try and warm him with her own heat.

After a while Ryan stopped shaking with unbearable cold and started to sweat instead. He tried to throw off the covers but Madeleine kept them pulled up tight to his neck. Later he seemed to sleep, so she got up and banked up the fire. By then it was afternoon and she lit every candle in the room in an attempt to hold back the pervading gloom. That day the coming twilight made her feel afraid, and that was something she never usually felt if Ryan was with her. His face was wet with sweat and his hair was curled and damp with it. It glistened on his black eyebrows and ran in salty pearls down his flushed cheeks. She dampened a rag in the washbasin and wiped his skin with it. He didn't respond when she spoke to him.

By then the bedclothes were wet, and she was very afraid of the intensity of heat pouring from his body. He got restless, constantly pushing at the covers, and he mumbled to himself, whispering names and words she didn't understand. His eyes were still closed, but he didn't seem to be truly asleep, at least not peacefully so. She sat on the bed and cradled his head in her lap. He seemed to know she was there and he snuggled against her for comfort. She leaned down and gently brushed his lips with hers. They felt dry and fiery to the touch. She didn't know what else to do for him. Then she remembered the herbal infusion Nancy had once shown her. It was supposed to help cool a fever. She got down from the bed and with an anxious glance back to where Ryan lay, went down to the kitchen and set to work.

It took her a little over an hour to prepare the drink, and as soon as it was ready she hurried back to him. The flickering candles showed her that he wasn't in the bed, but was curled up on the rug in front of the fire. He was shivering uncontrollably again and had obviously crawled to the fire to try and get warm. He woke at Madeleine's presence and told her that his head was hurting, that his throat felt raw. She gave him the drink she'd prepared and he drank it gratefully, though he was barely able to hold the cup steady because he was shaking so much. The drink seemed to soothe him and he subsided with a sigh. She fetched a blanket, and wrapped it around him, and then she lay down with him once more to warm him.

Just at that moment, the bedroom door suddenly flew open without even an enquiry or a knock, and Margaret stormed into the room. Madeleine sprang to her feet, angered and shocked at her stepmother's abrupt appearance.

"What is it?" she asked.

"What is it?" Margaret repeated. "The entire farm is falling into ruin with so many confined to their sick beds, and I find him here with you, like this! And you ask what is it?" She strode towards them. "You!" she pointed at Ryan. "You take too much advantage of our kindness to you! You spend time here with our daughter, teaching her your vile ways while others work!"

"Stepmother!" Madeleine shouted to silence her, "Ryan is ill! He made his condition worse than it need have been saving your stock from harm. Haven't you any compassion at all? Leave him be!"

"So, you hide behind a woman's skirt. Get up! Stand on your own two feet for once in your miserable existence!"

Ryan struggled to get up on shaky legs, bracing himself against the fire wall.

Madeleine turned back to him, "No." She knew that the illness was confusing him so that he was letting Margaret goad him. Madeleine put out a hand, which he was forced to grasp, as he would have fallen without it. He couldn't stand for more than a moment, and despite the support from her hand, he sagged against the wall, his legs betraying him. The rug started to slip from him and, to save him from final humiliation Madeleine clutched it quickly and wrapped it around him more securely.

"Stepmother…" she said, eyeing the woman coldly, "…leave us now for I am sure we wouldn't be welcome in your chambers."

With a contemptuous toss of her head Margaret left the room, slamming the door behind her with all her might.

Ryan collapsed back onto the rugs, his pent-up breath rasping from him. He rubbed his hand wearily over his aching head. Madeleine held him in her arms, stroking his temples to try and ease the pain, which was made worse by the fact that he still shuddered with chill. She pulled his damp hair from around his neck, feeling the skin there sticky with moisture. As soon as he slept again, she fetched fresh bed linen and remade the bed, so that she could help him into it for the night. Twice more he awoke in discomfort, and the infusion, though cold by then helped him back into a healing sleep.

CHAPTER FIFTEEN

It was as well that by the following spring, Ryan had regained his full strength, because there was trouble for Sarah's daughter, Emily. Mother and daughter came to the house to visit Sarah's sister Nancy. As soon as they walked into the kitchen that day, where Nancy and Madeleine were sitting preparing vegetables at the big table, it was obvious that something terrible had happened. Emily's face was black and yellow with bruising, and Sarah's eyes were puffy and red from crying. Sarah was a widow, little Emily born to her late in life, and they both worked at the nearby Chalfont household.

Emily was only twelve years old, and a young man called James, the son of the neighbouring Chalfont estate, had raped her. This had put both Emily and Sarah in a dreadful position, as well as being traumatic for them both. If Sarah had tried to complain about the disgraceful act, she would have lost her job and her home, and she would have become unemployable. Other employers would have shied away from the possible stigma.

James, who was twenty-two, had come across Emily alone in their farm dairy, after milking had ended. He had cornered her and mercilessly beaten her when she tried to resist his sexual attack. The outlook was inevitable; he had torn her clothes from the young girl and raped her. She'd been left there for her mother to find, battered, naked, and bleeding on the stone floor.

When Sarah brought Emily to the house that day, it was two weeks after the attack had taken place. It was the first opportunity she'd found to get away from the estate. Naturally she'd brought

Emily with her, for she was afraid to let the child out of her sight. Emily was traumatised. The worst thing, in Sarah's eyes, was that Emily was now totally terrified of all men, and couldn't bear any man near her. This made the future look very bleak, and not only in the workplace, where most employers would be men. Emily was very pretty, and Sarah had thought she might marry well. The child had been so badly hurt and abused, that Sarah feared she would never recover enough to live a normal life.

Madeleine sat and listened and didn't have any idea how to help. Two hours later the little girl's trauma was easy to see, because when Ryan came in for his supper, Emily was obviously petrified of him, even though he had never laid a finger on her. Acting and looking more like a four-year-old, she mewled pitifully and hid behind her mother. Ryan knew nothing of what had happened, but seeing Emily's fear, he was careful to keep the table between them, and didn't look directly at her. He sat down quietly and ate his supper.

Sarah explained to her sister Nancy that she hoped to leave Emily with her for a few days, because she was really frightened that having got away with it once, James was liable to try again. Nancy agreed, and after a while, because Ryan took no notice of her, Emily became a bit calmer and allowed her mother to go and leave her with her Aunt Nancy. After they had gone up to their bedroom, Madeleine told Ryan what had happened to Emily. To the likes of James Chalfont, Emily only existed to serve his every desire, because he considered himself superior to her, and that kind of behaviour always annoyed Ryan. It could sometimes make him reckless.

Emily reminded Ryan of his little sister, Beth, and that made what had happened to her even worse. He was determined to both help her, and to make Chalfont sorry he'd ever touched her. He was very careful all the next day to move very slowly and gently around Emily, as she clung to Nancy's skirt. If he ever caught her looking at him he was careful to smile just a little at her, crinkling his eyes to make the smile warm.

Later that day he set off to confront Chalfont. The bully became the bullied. Ryan had always been tall, strong, and bulky, but by this year he had filled out even more, and he made a formidable sight, clad in his anger. He skulked around the farm buildings until he managed to get the son of the house on his own. That James turned out to be a coward was no surprise, and he quickly collapsed in tears when Ryan pushed him bodily up against a wall and kneed him in the groin.

"There's no need to hurt me," Chalfont had whimpered.

"Don't stick your cock where it doesn't belong, or next time I'll cut it off!" was Ryan's cold threat. "Touch that child again, and I'll be back, you can count on it!"

"All right, all right," Chalfont snivelled, "Want her for yourself, do you?"

Ryan roared in fury and only just stopped himself from strangling the young man there and then. "You're an animal, Chalfont, not fit to live with pigs! If you don't want gutting like one of them, stay away from young girls!" Ryan left hurriedly, before his temper could get the better of him. If he'd beaten Chalfont, like he sorely wanted to, he would have been thrown in prison and left to rot. The rich, as always, had the best of the law.

By the time he got back to the house in Hambledon, he had hatched a plan. He picked a small posy of flowers from the garden and walked slowly into the kitchen. Emily was sitting in the big chair with the arms, looking very young and small in its oak embrace. Her little hands tightened their grip on the wooden arms when Ryan came in, but she stayed where she was and didn't run. He gave her the most courtly of bows, sweeping his arm out to the side. Then he presented her with the posy from the garden, which after a moment's hesitation, she reached out and took, shyly. Ryan was hoping that her mother would have told her magical fairy stories about knights and princesses, and that through the language of gallantry he would find a way to reach her damaged heart.

"My Lady Emily," he said, "May I have a moment to speak with you?"

She looked puzzled, but not too afraid, "Yes," she answered, in a whisper, a small frown wrinkling her brow.

Ryan got down on one knee in front of her, lessening his size so as to retain her frail confidence in him. Then he reached out his hand very slowly, as if she were a nervous colt, and gently took her hand in his.

"From this day forth, My Lady, I will be your champion. If you're ever under threat, call on me and I'll defend you. Don't fear any man, for I'll exact a fearful vengeance on any who cause you harm. Let everyone know that this is so. As for My Lady's sworn enemy, James Chalfont…" Emily flinched slightly at the mention of his name, and gripped Ryan's hand tighter, "…he is now also *my* enemy, and this he knows. He knows that he dare not ever harm My Lady Emily, for my revenge against him would be swift and sure. Have no more fear of him for he's a coward and a scoundrel."

It seemed to be working. Emily was smiling delightedly, and Ryan felt a small surge of triumph.

The next day was a holiday, so Madeleine and Ryan asked Emily to go with them on a picnic. She seemed to be a very different young lady already from the one that had arrived at house only days previously, and she agreed happily. During the outing, Ryan won her over completely by treating her the whole time as if she were a princess, lifting her carefully onto and off her horse, and fetching and carrying for her in a completely humble manner. And all day, he deliberately made a fool of himself, crawling after her on his knees, being deliberately clumsy and then humble, begging her forgiveness, until Emily even began to laugh at him. He knew then that he could really change things for her.

He was down on his knees in front of her, encouraging her to play the part of a princess, while he was her loyal and adoring servant. She suddenly froze, looking deep into his eyes, and he knew this was the moment of crisis, where she would come back from the awful dark place Chalfont had sent her, or, if Ryan made the wrong move, she would retreat forever into her shell. He didn't move at all, just stared levelly back at her, meeting her eyes with his, clearly and openly, hiding nothing. After a few moments when he felt his actual soul had been stripped bare by her eyes, she suddenly threw her arms around his neck and clung to him. Sarah had told them that Emily had never once cried after the attack, but she cried now. Sobs burst from the very centre of her being. Ryan wrapped his arms around her and held her, but not like a baby. He held her like the fledgling woman she was, tenderly but with respect and strength. She cried and cried until her tears had trickled down his neck and soaked into the shoulder of his shirt.

When Emily finally drew back, it was obvious from her happy expression that her heart was opening to being a happy child again. Ryan was ecstatic, having scored a winning point against a rich and uncaring man. When Sarah came to collect her daughter that evening, she was astounded and grateful to find her standing next to Ryan where he sat, seemingly totally unafraid. He had his arm around Emily's waist, and she leaned comfortably against him, her arm companionably laid across his shoulders.

As Sarah and her daughter left, Emily said in parting, "Goodbye Sir Ryan, my good Knight."

"Farewell, My Lady Emily," Ryan responded, then made her giggle by adding, "May the days pass swiftly until my eyes behold your beauty once more."

Ryan would have been seen as foolish by some people. He made enemies of rich, powerful people, and never seemed to care. James Chalfont might have been cowed by him enough to never hurt Emily again, but he was quite powerful, and the incident wouldn't have stopped him plotting against Ryan and conspiring with other enemies on ways to get rid of him.

Ryan managed to alienate another townsman one day, less powerful and certainly not rich, but a man who knew enough fellow thugs to become a problem if he chose to. His name was Jed Cooper.

Jed was a drunk, but as most people drank ale rather than water for hygiene reasons, he wasn't unusual. When Jed got really drunk though, he became violent towards his wife, Joy, and on extreme occasions, his son, Noah. It usually went on behind closed doors but it was known. Ryan had often seen Jed drunk of course, as had everyone in the town, but this day it took a more sinister turn, and in a way that he couldn't in conscience, ignore. It was a Tuesday, the regular market day, so the town was busy, and any commoners who could afford to be drunk, were.

Ryan and Madeleine were walking through the town together, arm in arm. They passed by the inn in the High Street, on their way up to the church, just as Jed came out. He was reeling around and aggressive, and the couple crossed the road to avoid walking next to him. They thought little more about it, as they had been on their way to the churchyard so that Madeleine could visit the grave of her mother, Rebecca. By the time they came back down the street and turned left at the bottom of the hill, there was a commotion going on outside one of the cottages. Jed's wife, Joy, was outside, screaming and hammering on the cottage door.

"Jed! For the love of God, no! Leave him be! Let me in!"

Naturally a small group of people was gathering, curious as to what was going on, but none would intervene, except Ryan. He took hold of the sobbing, hysterical woman by her shoulders and turned her away from the door. Her screaming stopped abruptly as she faced him.

"What is it? What's wrong?" he asked her quietly.

"It's Jed, he's drunk. He grabbed Noah and threw me out of the house." she sobbed, her voice breaking. "What's he going to do to my son?"

Ryan hammered on the door himself, "Jed! Open it or I'll break it in!" He hammered harder for a few moments, "You have five seconds to open this door!" He stopped banging and there was a brief silence, then the door opened an inch. Ryan immediately shoved it as hard as he could, catching the drunken Jed off guard, and the door flew open. A small figure dashed out, closely followed by Jed.

"C'mere you!" he yelled, clutching at Noah with an outstretched arm.

The boy fled behind Ryan and Joy, peering out. Ryan grabbed Jed with both hands, gripping his upper arms tightly, and the man was brought to a sudden halt. "You and I need to have a little talk," Ryan suggested to the suddenly immobile Jed.

"No," said Jed, "We don't! That's my boy and I'll…" He stopped as Ryan's grip tightened, "Ow! Leave off!"

Ryan backed the man up, through the front door, away from prying eyes, and shut the door behind them.

The small crowd, including Noah, Joy, and Madeleine, waited expectantly to see what would happen next in this riveting drama. Some of the town men and women started muttering among themselves, and Madeleine grew a little anxious as they made it obvious that they were expecting fireworks from the two men. But, as time passed, there was no noise at all from the house, let alone any sounds of fighting. The crowd grew restless, but still there was only silence from within. They started to get bored and most wanted to get back to the market and their work, so gradually they drifted away.

Ryan must have been waiting for them to go, to lessen the explosiveness of the situation, because no sooner had the last one left than the door opened and he walked out. Sheepish, and apparently sobered, Jed followed him out.

He looked to his wife and son, "Come on boy, in you come. You too, Joy."

Joy and Noah looked at Ryan, their eyes wide, "It's all right," he assured them nodding, "You can go in. He's not going to hurt you, are you Jed?"

Jed glanced anxiously at Ryan, "No, no, never."

Joy and Noah walked past Ryan and went into the house. Joy patted Ryan's arm as she walked past him.

The door closed, and all was quiet.

"What happened?" Madeleine wanted to know.

"Nothing much. We just had a little talk about family," was all Ryan would say.

So while Joy and Noah had been completely won over, Jed would no doubt have been another matter. There were several incidents such as this. For instance, one time Ryan stood up for the Oswald family against their landlords. It just wasn't done in those days, and anyone who stepped out of line like that had many queuing up to take their revenge one day…

CHAPTER SIXTEEN

A s the months passed, Margaret struggled to find ways to rid herself of her unwanted son-in-law. There were many times when she almost decided to send an assassin after him with a good sharp knife, but she was too scared to do it. Edwin mostly took her side, but he could be unpredictable, and if he found that she had instigated a murder, she might find herself out on the streets. She had to always use some degree of subtlety. There was a young man called Robert Symons. He would never have been Margaret's first choice to marry Madeleine, having none of the money or influence that Pennington had, but he might be useful. He was big, tall, strong and young, and a physical match for Fitzgerald. Maybe he could be goaded into committing the murder for her.

Knowing that Robert was besotted with Madeleine, Margaret sent word to him that her stepdaughter had asked to see him. The inference in her message was that now he might be accepted by her as a future husband. Margaret made no mention of the fact that Madeleine had already married, of course. Robert arrived within hours of the message being sent, and Margaret welcomed him with open arms, still not being specific about the situation, just leading him gently on. It almost worked.

Full of young passion and ardour, Robert rushed down to the bridge, where Margaret had told him that Madeleine would be waiting. She didn't tell him that she would be waiting for her husband there. Robert found Madeleine sitting on the narrow parapet, where she was watching for Ryan. When the young man almost immediately dropped down on one knee, it was obvious what his intention was, and Madeleine stared at him, horrified. He clutched her hand while she was still trying to find the right words. But before he could actually begin to speak, his attention was drawn sharply to something off to one side of the bridge.

Ryan stood there, his arms folded across his chest, with his brows raised and a slight smile on his lips, waiting there with apparent interest to see what was to happen.

"Madeleine," Robert asked, "who is that?"

"Robert, I'm sorry to disappoint you, but this is my husband, Ryan Fitzgerald."

Robert snarled, jumping to his feet, growing red in the face, "Your husband!" he shouted, "This commoner! I don't believe it! Are you trying to make a fool of me? I was told…"

"I'm sorry…" Madeleine began, but he interrupted her.

"Nobody will make a fool of me; else they'll live to regret it!" Then he grasped her wrist and pulled her to her feet, and close up to him.

Ryan suddenly became serious and hurried forward, taking hold of Madeleine's shoulders from behind, and turning her aside, out of harm's way.

Then he stood between them, "I *am* Madeleine's husband," he said with quiet authority.

"No!" Robert couldn't accept it. He grabbed hold of Ryan's shirt with both hands and shoved him back roughly. Ryan shoved his arms between Robert's and took hold of his shirt too, shoving him backwards with equal force. They were, as Margaret had hoped, equally matched in height and weight, and they pushed each other back and forth across the narrow bridge. Then Ryan, with a grunt of effort, forced Robert backwards until he crashed into the bridge's guard-rail, which creaked alarmingly. For a moment it seemed as if the rail would break and both men would plummet down into the stream twenty feet below.

In the end it was only Robert who fell. He swung a wild punch at Ryan just as the rail snapped, and it unbalanced him, so that he tumbled into space. He just managed to catch hold of the edge of the bridge. He would have soon fallen though, had Ryan not grasped his arm, and held him fast until he could climb back to safety. Even once he was safe, Robert leapt to his feet, and once more stood eye to eye with Ryan, unable to back down. He suddenly reached down to his boot and came up with a wicked looking knife in his fist. Up to that point Madeleine had felt some sympathy for Robert because he'd obviously been misled by Margaret, and now he didn't know how to back down with his pride intact, but a knife in his hand changed things.

She pushed between the two men, and strongly resisted Ryan's attempts to make her move out of the way. There wasn't much he could do unless he became rough with her, and she knew he wouldn't do that. She looked Robert squarely in the eye.

"I'm very fond of you Robert, and I'm really sorry," she said. "Our marriage has caused great discord in the family, so it hasn't been made public knowledge. I would never belittle you, please...don't make it worse with violence. It was *her* who tried to make a fool of you, not us."

Robert snarled, glaring at her, and then turned and walked away without another word.

Margaret was absolutely furious when she learned that her plot had failed. That damn Irishman, he must have a pact with the devil, because he certainly had the devil's luck! She decided to try a yet more subtle avenue of attack. If violence didn't work, then she would try seduction. She knew that Ryan had been sharing many different beds before marrying Madeleine and 'apparently' restricting himself to just one. He obviously had the morals of an alley cat, so it shouldn't be too difficult to snare him, and she knew just the person to do it. She knew that Madeleine would never be able to forgive infidelity, and she was certain this time her plan would work. She sat down and composed a letter to her good friend, Evelyn.

When Margaret and another well-to-do woman passed through the kitchen gardens where he was busy digging, Ryan had no idea that a trap was forming around him. Evelyn was a very beautiful lady with red hair and green eyes. At the moment they were passing, Ryan was crouched down, prising a large stone out of the soil with his hands so that he could continue digging. Evelyn paused at the end of the vegetable bed, and Ryan glanced sidelong up at them, curious as to why they were looking at him so intently. Evelyn met Ryan's gaze and held it.

After a brief, muttered conversation with Evelyn, Margaret appeared to hurry her along, and the two women went into the house. Ryan shrugged, *odd,* he thought, and carried on working.

Some time later, Margaret reappeared at Ryan's side, and warned him off talking to Evelyn. He was mystified, because something in her manner made him feel that she was almost daring him to deny her, encouraging him even, but didn't think it to be of any consequence. Two hours later, when Ryan was in the loft of the big barn, stacking hay, Evelyn came to him. She hitched up her skirts in a most unladylike manner, and climbed the ladder up to him.

As she arrived in the loft, smoothing out her skirt, Ryan

continued to work, but as a servant should do, he asked her, "Can I help you, my Lady?"

"Yes, I believe you can," she replied, stepping up close to him, and laying her hand on the pitchfork so that he was forced to stop work. "What's your name?"

"Ryan," he replied, feeling a bit uneasy. Something was going on, but what?

"Well, Ryan, there's a service I require of you. A service I am sure you'll enjoy. Come with me at once to my bedchamber." She met his shocked eyes unashamedly, her own green eyes gleaming as she left him in no doubt as to her requirements of him.

"I'm sorry, my Lady, I can't," he replied, folding his arms across his chest in a defensive gesture, and wondering how he could get out of the situation without causing offence. "In any case, I wouldn't be permitted in that part of the house."

She placed a hand softly on each of his forearms, saying, "The place does not matter." Her green eyes grew soft and her lashes lowered. "This place will suffice as well as anywhere. It's warm and comfortable," she purred, eyeing the soft piles of hay, "There's no-one to see us."

Ryan dropped his hands to his sides, so that her hands fell from him. "I'm sorry, I can't," he repeated. "I've a great deal of work that must be done before dark." He was flummoxed, mystified, and not sure how to react to stop her. He was reluctant to say that he was Madeleine's husband too, because he was sure that some plan of Margaret's was being carried out here, and he was afraid of falling into whatever trap she had laid. He wanted to keep Madeleine out of it, whatever it was.

Evelyn stepped even closer, her high breasts brushing against him, and she looked up at him, her eyes hungry, her lips slightly parted.

After a pause she replied, "You misunderstand me, this is not a request; it is an order." She put her arms around his neck, stretched up on her toes and lifted her mouth to his. But he drew his head back out of reach, and gently took hold of her wrists, pulling her arms from his neck.

"I'm married," he pointed out, showing her the ring on his finger, hoping that would be the end of it.

"That is no concern of mine," she responded, sounding a little angry. Then her tone softened, "Listen, I am married too, but my husband's an impotent and infertile man. I must have a child. Time is running out for me." She paused, "Your eyes are such a remarkable colour. I'd love to have a child with your eyes. I don't require your future or your allegiance, only your seed. I'm told I am beautiful, and no doubt you are married to some fat peasant, so how can you refuse me? Come..." she tried to lead him deeper into the lengthening shadows, but he resisted her.

"You truly are a beautiful woman, but my wife is equally beautiful, and I love her. We've taken and given a vow, which will never be broken. Please, I ask you to respect it."

She was a little taken aback at this declaration, and she said, "Even if I tell you that I will make certain you lose your position here?"

"Yes."

"Even if I swear that your wife would never know?"

"Yes."

"Then this peasant wife of yours is very fortunate, and I hope she understands her good fortune..." She left the sentence hanging, and a little wistfully, trailed a finger-tip down Ryan's chest, before she turned and left the barn.

Later, Ryan didn't know what to do about what had happened in the barn. If he tried to explain to Madeleine, she might get hold of the wrong end of the stick, and if he didn't tell her, then somebody else might. He was in turmoil, terrified that Madeleine would think he'd betrayed her, when nothing could have been further from the truth.

He met her in the walled garden, stepped up close against her and rested his arms lightly across her shoulders, lacing his fingers together loosely at the nape of her neck. Their eyes were inches apart, blue on blue.

"What is it?" she prompted.

"Something happened this afternoon..." he hesitated, "Well, in fact nothing really happened. But I'm concerned that word might get back to you, either through Evelyn, for she doesn't know that you're my wife, or from another more malicious source, if she finds out from Evelyn."

"You mean my stepmother?"

"Yes, Madeleine, I do."

"She could say nothing bad about you that I'd believe. You know that's been tried before."

"But this time Evelyn might...they might conspire together to convince you..." His voice petered out, and he unlaced his hands, cupping her face in them tenderly, his eyes intense.

"Ryan, what's happened? You must tell me yourself, so that there's no misunderstanding."

His eyes dropped; he was embarrassed, and he spoke with downcast eyes.

"It seems that Evelyn had chosen me to father her child." His eyes lifted searchingly to hers once more, anxious to gauge her reaction to his revelation.

Madeleine frowned, "My God...so what happened?"

"Nothing happened; I refused her. You know I'd never..."

"But what happened? What did she do? Tell me!" she insisted.

"Very well...all right," Ryan raised his hands in appeasement, thinking that she was angry. He didn't relish telling her the details, but he knew she had to know the whole truth.

"Evelyn came to me when I was alone in the loft over the barn, and asked, no demanded, that I lie with her."

"And...?"

"Madeleine!" he exclaimed, "You know that I'd never betray you."

She laid her hands against his chest and smiled up at his worried face, "I know you wouldn't. I'm teasing you."

He let out a long sigh of relief and hugged her to him, her hands now captive between them. "She told me, when I refused her, that she'd tell your mother, in order that I'd be dismissed, and I was afraid that your mother would then come to you with a lie."

"How did she try to tempt you?" Madeleine asked.

Eventually she drew it out of him, all of it, the touching, the attempted kiss, the soft persuasive words, and the threats and promises. Madeleine stood back, an expression of sheer indignation on her face, "How dare she put her hands on you?"

Ryan felt the tension in her body, and took her face in his hands again so that their eyes met, "Nothing would ever tempt me. I'll always be only yours. When I found you I found everything I have ever wanted. I will never hurt you, and I wouldn't risk the horror of losing you just for the sake of a brief moment of pleasure. And when it comes to you, only you, I'll stop at nothing to make you happy. No one else will ever matter to me."

He embraced her with his eyes, and her angry expression faded a little, "All the same. Even if I had been the fat peasant she expected, it would have been just as bad for me that she would steal you. How dare she?"

Ryan started to run his hands up and down her back and she softened into his arms.

At that moment Margaret stalked into view, and had obviously been eavesdropping. "What do you mean, how dare *she*?" she demanded, "Your 'husband' has assaulted my friend!"

Madeleine just laughed, "Don't be ridiculous!" She stretched up to Ryan and kissed him passionately, as if no-one but he was there at all.

CHAPTER SEVENTEEN

Spring soon came around and with it the first anniversary of Ryan and Madeleine's wedding. Madeleine had wanted to find Ryan a present to mark the occasion, something special and personal. She had no money because her parents had not allowed her any since she had married Ryan, and he got only his keep in exchange for his work. Nancy came to the rescue as she had often done in the past. Madeleine had a dark blue silky gown that she never wore, and so Nancy cut it up and made it into a new shirt for Ryan. The colour suited him perfectly.

Ryan had kept a secret from Madeleine. He'd been doing extra work in the village for the whole year that they had been married and had scraped together enough money to buy her a gold wedding ring to replace the one that Nancy had lent her. The entwined initials R and M were engraved on it. Madeleine was speechless when she saw it, but there was still another surprise. Ryan took her down to the woods at twilight and to the big oak that they considered to be their special tree. He had put candles in the branches, probably fifty or more, and they twinkled like earthbound stars, lighting the grove like a fairyland village. He'd also laid a fire, which he lit, and they sat on rugs from the house, sipping wine and staring into the flickering flames. Soon they lay down together in the shimmering light.

1639 was a very special time in both their lives. In the early summer they had another rare and wonderful day when everything seemed perfect. There was magic in the air, right from the early morning when they set off. Pearly, pink mist was kissing the gardens with a rosy glow. It gave Madeleine such a mystical feeling that she wouldn't have been surprised to see a unicorn come prancing out of the dawn. They left the house before anyone else had risen, except for a few servants. Nancy had packed them a basket of food so that they would be able to spend the whole day alone.

They were excited at the prospect of the day together, exploring unknown reaches of the Forest of Bere. They rode for several hours, until the sun had risen up high above them, and had started to make both the horses and their riders hot and sweaty. They came to a clearing that they had never seen before, and were almost speechless at the beauty of it. The ground sloped down to a bubbling stream. It was crystal clear and ran deep in places over large rocks. In one place the rocks had formed a natural pool, which foamed and swirled as the water tried to escape from its prison. There were some smaller trees there, young oaks and beeches struggling for life in the cool shade of their mightier ancestors. However, there was a gap in the leafy canopy overhead, just above the water, and the sun was high enough to shine directly down on the pool, filling it with glittering flashes of light. The grass at the side of the stream was soft and mossy, warm and inviting.

They walked the horses into the stream to cool their legs, and then left them loose to graze nearby. They seemed quite content not to roam too far, perhaps affected by the sense of peace that seemed to fill the glade. Madeleine was embarrassed at Ryan's suggestion that they take off their clothes and bathe in the pool, not used to the feel of the air on her bare skin. Still, she soon followed his example as he stripped naked and jumped straight into the whirling pool. The delicious feeling of the water lashing against her skin was irresistible, as was its invasion of every corner of her body with its cool, gentle fingers. After a while they were chilled, and so they climbed back up to the bank and wrapped themselves in their cloaks, to eat their food. Starting to feel warmer, they snuggled up, tangled together like puppies.

Madeleine fell asleep. She dreamed that she awoke to find Ryan gone, and suddenly leapt from sleep with a cry on her lips. Ryan was not at her side. She looked around frantically, and there he was, standing naked atop a large rock where it jutted from the water. She gasped, both at his temerity, and at the wonderful sight he made. He didn't hear her at first above the sound of the stream, and she was able to sit and watch him secretly for a while.

She'd discovered that it was considered entirely improper for a lady to admire the body of a man. She'd found this out quite innocently a few days after the consummation of their marriage when being advised by the older married women. They'd been shocked numb by her comments of how she loved to lie with Ryan. They were totally horror-stricken when she asked them if they too found their husbands' parts delightful. So she took quiet, sinful pleasure in imagining their faces, if they could have only known what she was thinking at that moment. She called out to Ryan, overcome with desire, and wanting him to come to her.

He jumped from rock to rock, and then landed on the bank, seemingly quite unconscious of the spectacle he was creating. He ran to her where she sat. She tried to draw him down to her, but instead he stayed standing, pulled off her cloak, and pushed her down. Then he stood astride her naked body. He lowered himself, pushing his knees between hers, and he began to stroke her secret places softly, over and over, until she could barely stand it. She wondered, with a gentle smile, what the ladies of the house would think if they could see them now, totally, unashamedly, enjoying the sight and touch of each other. The glade had such a hold on them that they didn't leave it until it was almost too late to get home before dark.

In high summer that year a tragedy struck the area. A large tract of the forest and at least one house was burned down as fire took hold and raced through the dry greenery. When the fire was first spotted, all the able-bodied among the staff from all the houses nearby were sent to try and help. Ryan was just one such among those from their house. The alarm had gone off at 4am and he had left Madeleine asleep in their bed. They all rode, ran, and drove in carts, to the house where the fire had started, but by then there was little they could do. The only survivor was one dog, all the people having died in their beds. It was likely that the thatched roof of the house had been smouldering all night; so that when the fire finally broke free it was fast and hot and unstoppable, consuming the upper floor very quickly.

The problem then was that the embers had set fire to the nearby brush, which in turn had spread to the dry tops of the trees. By the time people got to the house, the forest itself was already well alight, and the wind was driving the flames and smoke towards the west. Chaos reigned, with some people looting the burnt house remains, and others fetching what little water they could from the well to try and douse the fallen burning timbers that still glowed with incredible heat. It was all pointless.

Finally, someone took charge and it was decided that a firebreak should be made ahead of the fire. The older people and the women were sent back to their various places of work, while the younger men were sent off to start cutting a firebreak. To do this they had to go around the fire on the eastern side to avoid getting trapped by it.

Nancy was among those sent back to the de Port house, and once there she met a very worried Madeleine, whose main concern, as always, was what had happened to Ryan. Nancy was exhausted, but reassured the girl that Ryan had been fine last time she had seen him, and that he had gone with the others to cut a firebreak in the forest to try and stop the fire by starving it of fuel. Madeleine was determined to go and find him, and although her father and Nancy forbade her to, after a while she couldn't stand waiting any longer. She snuck into the stables and took a horse, riding off towards the smoke she could see curling above the treetops like a giant bird of prey in the distant sky.

Ryan worked for hours, soot and smoke making him cough as it seeped into his lungs. It was the same for everyone. Using hatchets, axes, saws and their bare hands they widened a natural pathway so that the fire would have too big a gap to jump when it got there. The firebreak worked, and a ragged cheer went up when it became obvious that the fire was dying back. Then the wind changed violently, and the flames grew higher again, pushing back towards the east. The prevailing winds were always from the south-west, so this was always something that was likely to happen. The men at the break could do no more, and a contingent from the villages now in the path of the fire would be forming their own firebreak in that direction. Eventually the fire would be penned in and starved into submission. Ryan and his group were given leave to go home. It was a long tiring walk all the way back to Hambledon.

When Ryan reached the yard of the house he was met by Nancy and Edwin, who had just discovered Madeleine's absence, and they were both in a state of panic. Ryan's weariness fled on wings of fear as they told him that she had been gone for at least an hour. Most dreadful, the horse she had taken had come back on its own, rider-less, minutes before Ryan had arrived. Saddling Edwin's best horse, with Madeleine's father for once having no objection, Ryan mounted, and set off at a gallop back towards the burnt-out house.

When he reached it, he was told that Madeleine had headed east, which at the time had been safe, but as he knew, was now directly in the path of the fire. As he rode closer and closer to the seat of the wildfire, his horse started to spook badly, trying to jink back the way it had come, rearing and spinning. He drove it on furiously with hand and leg, knowing that if he was unseated, both he and Madeleine would be lost.

Time and again as the smoke thickened, he thought he could see her ahead of him, but the shapes he saw always turned out to be just smoke ghosts. Flames were licking the grass around the horse's hooves, but luckily it was still moist enough not to burst into flames. The horse squealed and pranced, trying to run away, but Ryan kept it moving forward, even though he was almost giving up hope of finding Madeleine, or even getting out alive himself. There was no choice though, he had to just pray and keep going. There was no going back without her, because if he did he would be returning to an empty, dark world, and he would rather die in the flames than go back to that place.

As he rode, he marvelled at how things had changed for him. The road no longer beckoned as it had when he first arrived in England. He couldn't run anymore, because if he did now, he'd be running away from love, instead of away from fear. She'd tamed him, like no other woman had been able to do. He didn't know how because his mind was beyond reasoning when it came to her. Where was she? He pulled the horse to a stop, to see if he could hear anything, but it was hopeless. The horse wouldn't keep still for a start, and the roar of the fire was so close now that it drowned out everything else. He moved on. The horse's coat was smutty with soot, dark with sweat, and grey with ash, and he expected that his face looked the same. He decided to put his trust in God and in his strong connection to his wife, relaxed his hands a little on the reins, and just followed his heart, calling out her name. His soul cried out silently to hers.

Minutes later when his throat was too parched and raw for him to shout any longer he suddenly heard a faint cry. Someone was screaming as if they were being burnt alive. He kicked the horse forwards with everything he had left, and the animal responded, charging between two burning bushes. There she was, staggering around blindly in the smoke. He rode up to her and reached down, grabbing her around the waist and heaving her bodily up onto the horse in front of him. She knew it was him, gasping his name in total disbelief that he had come for her, and that he had found her. He turned the horse at last in the direction it wanted to go and gave it its head, still steering it forcefully around tree branches that they could not safely pass under. Foam flew from the horse's mouth as it sped on its way, with the two of them clinging desperately to its back.

The flight from the fire seemed to take forever, and Ryan was feeling the strain of all his efforts, but finally they reached clean air, and he began to hope that they would be safe. The horse seemed to feel it too, and gradually the exhausted animal slowed from a gallop to a trot, to a walk, to a standstill. It could go no further with its double burden. The fight and the fear and the flight had totally depleted it, and it staggered as it stopped, almost collapsing. Ryan almost fell from its back, and held up trembling arms to catch Madeleine. But his strength gave out as he took her weight, and he sank to the ground on rubber legs, with her on his lap. They stayed that way for a long time, neither able to speak, and the horse standing, panting, head down, before they finally found the strength to set off for home. As they walked, Madeleine explained that her horse had become impossible to control, and that eventually she'd dismounted, because she'd been afraid it would take her into the fire in its panic. Of course as soon as she had loosed her grip on the reins it had taken off and quickly disappeared. She was glad to hear it had reached home safely.

Just this once, when they got there, Ryan received a smile of gratitude and a handshake from Madeleine's father for rescuing her, but he knew that it meant nothing as regards his future, because Edwin was a weak man married to a strong woman. Margaret herself stayed out of sight, not wanting, Ryan presumed, to have to put on any kind of act. He had a nasty feeling that she would probably have willingly sacrificed her stepdaughter if it meant getting rid of him too. It was days before they got the smell of smoke and charred wood out of their skin and hair, but Ryan just thanked God that the time of his parting from Madeleine had not yet come.

CHAPTER EIGHTEEN

In September or October every year the annual apple-harvesting took place. This was a special day when all the apples were picked and made into cider. In that year, 1639, it took place in late September, because the weather was thought to be going to turn very wet after the very dry summer. It was necessary to get the crop in quickly because it would soon rot once the rain came.

Apple harvesting was always a happy time. Everyone, except Edwin and Margaret of course, joined in the task. Two ponies stood patiently in the shade, waiting for their carts to be filled with fruit, and every little while Madeleine would fetch the ponies an apple as a reward. Laughter filled the air, for this was easy work compared with the normal labours. Whole families toiled happily together, united in camaraderie with others and their families. Everyone was keenly anticipating the taste of the cider. Back in the dairy, preparations were under way for the pressing of the apples. Ryan and Madeleine were together in company that accepted them, and that was all they ever really needed to be happy.

The leaves on the apple trees in the orchard were just starting to lose their vitality. Their edges were dry and curling, gradually changing from green to brown. By contrast, the apples themselves shone with life, rosy and vibrant, as if they had sucked out all the vitality of the trees and locked it inside them. Some had fallen though, and lay chewed open, half-eaten by wasps and birds, their sweet juices drunk dry.

Ryan plucked the apples and handed them down to Madeleine, and she piled them into a wicker basket. When each basket was full,

Ryan carried it to one of the carts. At midday, servants brought a picnic lunch to the orchard, for everyone. This was the workers' payment for the day. There was no difference that day between the workers and the highborn among them, and that was one of the reasons why Ryan loved it so. He also loved the sense of belonging to one big family. Everyone sat on the grass to eat, leaning on the trees, and on each other. Ryan sat down, resting his back against one of the old gnarled trunks, and Madeleine lay outstretched, with her head on his lap. Sighing deeply, Ryan linked his hands behind his head and closed his eyes, an expression of sheer bliss on his face. *If only it could always be like this,* he thought.

Later in the afternoon when the picking was done, the trees stood bare of their juicy treasure, and the apples were all back at the dairy being pressed in readiness for their transformation into delicious cider, games were organised. The favourite among the children was apple bobbing. Tubs of water had apples floating in them, and the contestants had to keep their hands behind their backs while leaning forwards, trying to snatch an apple, using only their mouths and teeth.

Naturally the apples were pushed under the water during attempts to grab them, and everyone got very wet trying to capture the elusive trophies. Several of the children, giggling and egging each other on, and knowing that he would be a willing victim, approached Ryan. They grasped his hands and arms and pulled him, while he struggled in mock protest, over to the tubs. Once beside the bobbing apples, he entered fully into the spirit of things, plunging his head beneath the water. The trick, as he knew, was to push an apple right to the bottom of the tub, heedless of the water, and grip it against the bottom with your teeth.

He was greeted with gleeful shrieks from the children when he reared up from the tub, an apple clenched in his teeth, his hair soaking wet, spraying water droplets over them as he deliberately shook his head. He came back to Madeleine and presented her with his apple, then smiling, hugged her to him, deliberately soaking her too with his streaming wet hair and wet shirtfront. The children laughed as they watched his antics. His eyes were aglow with laughter, his hair plastered to his head, and his life force was bubbling so incandescently that he knew he was infecting everyone else with it. These were the kinds of days he lived for, when he had confidence that he was doing what he was meant to.

The children wanted play hide and go seek, and of course wanted Ryan to play with them. He agreed happily, enjoying the chance to regress to childhood, as always, and he and the children, all but one that was to 'seek', ran into the trees to hide. Madeleine was to help the seeker, and so after counting to the obligatory one hundred, they set off to find the others. Those in hiding had to try and make their way behind their backs to 'home', the orchard, before they were 'tagged'.

A lot of the children sneaked past Madeleine and the seeker and made it home, but most of the others we chased and tagged. Soon there was only one boy, and Ryan, who hadn't been found. The tagged children joined in the hunt, but all the hollow trees and other obvious hiding places had already been searched without finding the prey. A group of seekers were passing beneath an ancient oak when suddenly, and startlingly, Ryan dropped into sight, dangling upside down from the large branch. He had his legs hooked over the branch, and hung there, his hair loose and trailing towards the ground. In his arms he held the missing boy, who now dropped gleefully to the ground, and, taking advantage of the surprise, made off and ran 'home' to the orchard.

Ryan however, couldn't escape them. Willing hands reached for him as the children jumped up, grasping his arms, and soon, by the sheer weight of the number clinging to him, he was pulled from the tree. He landed sprawling on the ground, hidden momentarily by the squealing children as they swarmed triumphantly over him. Madeleine stood back while the excited young ones scrambled to their feet and pulled Ryan up too. Then she followed behind as they dragged their prize captive back to the orchard.

That evening Ryan and Madeleine decided to sleep under the stars. They collected some firewood and made a shelter out of poles and leafy branches in case in rained. But it was a beautiful night and they had no need of the shelter. There was only a tiny crescent moon so that the stars were dazzling, both in their brilliance and their number.

Madeleine came to Ryan naked, glowing golden in the light from the fire, backlit by a million crystal cold stars. She took Ryan's breath away as the scintillating lights caressed every curve and dip of her body. He lit another fire when he kissed her, his hands trailing gently and slowly down her back. Madeleine felt his hardness through his clothes, and smiled at her affect on him. By the time she had undressed him he was almost out of control with desire. He picked her up bodily; her legs wrapped around his waist, and carried her to a broad tree. Leaning her back against it, while keeping his arms around her to protect her skin from the rough bark, he entered her in a single, explosive, thrust.

Later they lay in contented exhaustion, side by side, looking up at the stars and gradually drifting into a peaceful sleep. They woke with the dawn, and watched the sky turn. First a faint yellow sliver that warmed through to peach, then to a pink and red fire, and then the sky itself transformed from a watery blue to deep cobalt, as the birds sung to welcome the day.

The winter months gave Margaret time to think of several schemes to part the couple. Her obsession was making her ill. She brooded over ways she believed Ryan had slighted her, and grew angry when she recalled times she had felt humiliated. She fed her anger, going over and over what she considered to be past insults. She was scornful of the love the couple seemed to share, and on the other hand...jealous. That was something that she would never admit though, not even to herself. She was determined to destroy the Irishman and Madeleine too, if that was what it took.

Back in the summer something had happened that still made her blood run cold when she thought of it. She hugged the incident to her, allowing it to nurture her hatred and obsession. She had always had a terrible fear of thunderstorms, which would send her spiralling into panic, and *he* had taken advantage of that fact. He had taken advantage of her fear in order to humiliate her.

Margaret had been out collecting flowers for her guests' table, a harmless enough occupation. She had wandered further than she had intended to, preoccupied with what she would talk to her guests about to impress them, and always going a few more steps in search of the perfect flower specimen. The clouds must have been brewing overhead, but the canopy of trees had hidden them, and although the air had grown humid, she thought her sweat was just due to the exercise, which she was not accustomed to. So she was totally shocked when a thunderclap rent the air, almost simultaneously accompanied by sudden torrential rain that soaked her to the skin in seconds, despite the cover of the trees overhead.

Terror shook her instantly. The loud noises took her back to her childhood, and she immediately felt like a frightened child again. She turned this way and that, but suddenly was unsure of the right direction to go back to the house. Paths that she'd known minutes before suddenly looked like strange silver-muddied trails that might lead anywhere. Lightning flashed, blinding her, and she ran to the nearest tree, falling down, clutching it, while her heart raced in her chest. Her breath was fast and shallow, and she got dizzy. The storm raged around her as her mind virtually left her. She became a gibbering wreck, unable to move from the tree. After what seemed like hours, a thunderbolt hit another tree nearby, her screams pealed out, and *thank God*, a figure was lit up by the accompanying lightning flash. She saw the person turning towards the sound of her voice. She didn't know who it was until he crouched down beside her and took her in his arms.

Then she knew, by the scent of him and by his voice. It was the accursed Irishman! She wanted desperately to push his hated presence away, and yet she was so deathly afraid that she had no alternative but to cling to him. She was disgusted with herself, but she knew that if she turned him away, she would die there, alone. *Why in God's name did it have to be him that found her?* She couldn't stand or even move, but clutched at his body, clawing through his shirt, trying to hide from the heavenly display overhead.

Gradually, with painful slowness, the storm eased off, and the rain decreased, until all that could be heard were cascades of water drips pouring from the leaves of the trees. It had been a very short rainstorm, typical of that summer. Her ears recovered from the thunder's onslaught and she became aware of birdsong starting up.

At last she was able to stand up. She screamed silently at her weak body though, because she still couldn't walk without clinging onto him; her worst enemy. The man she hated more than anyone in the world, and she was being forced to clutch him like a two-year old child, *or a lover*. That last thought was scrubbed from her mind the instant it was given birth to.

They reached the garden at last, and she could see sanctuary in the form of the front door of the house. Instantly, she pushed herself away from him.

She turned and sneered at him, shouting at his startled face, "Get off me! Let go of me!" He let go, and she marched up the steps and through the door, without a second glance at him. She knew he had found her on purpose, just to shame her, just to take advantage of her fear, and no persuasion from Edwin that it had been mere chance, and that all the men were out looking for her, would convince her otherwise.

She knew that it was far too late to try and pretend to the world that Madeleine's marriage had never happened, and marry her off to someone more suitable, but if the girl were to become *a widow*, things would be different.

CHAPTER NINETEEN

Margaret gradually grew more desperate in her attempts to get rid of Ryan, but often just to cause trouble between him and Madeleine was enough to keep her happy for weeks. Madeleine knew it was another of her stepmother's schemes when her step-cousins Dominic and Edward turned up one early December day. They had started coming to visit when Margaret first came into the family. They were nothing but rude aggressive bullies, and Madeleine had never liked them. Even when she was at an innocent age, she'd struggled to keep her honour when they were near, and she'd often felt in danger from them.

Dominic and Edward arrived in the morning, and they were nothing but trouble right from the first moment. Ryan was out working, so Madeleine kept to the kitchen, hoping to avoid them. But it wasn't to be. They appeared, smiling slyly, in the kitchen doorway. They slunk into the room like a pair of cur dogs, crowding against their younger cousin.

"Why Madeleine, my dear," Edward began with insolence, "how you have grown. You are truly a flower ready to be picked."

"Edward, Dominic," she greeted them with a curt nod. From the corner of her eye, she could see Nancy bristling like an affronted mother hen. But Nancy wouldn't dare intervene.

"Madeleine," Dominic said, impertinently stroking her cheek with one finger, "our good aunt tells us that you have married below your station. An Irish peasant, isn't it?"

"Ryan is no peasant," she retorted.

"But, surely, he's just a boy?" Edward said. "Dominic and I could perhaps give him some advice on matters that only men know of."

Madeleine snorted, unable to hide her contempt. The thought of those buffoons instructing Ryan on the manly arts was laughable.

"Are you laughing at us, Madeleine?" Edward's voice had taken a dangerous tilt, his eyes narrowing.

"No," she protested, "of course not, but I have to go. I've duties elsewhere." Swiftly, she left the kitchen, and ran upstairs to hide behind the safety of her locked bedroom door.

At noon, feeling safer, Madeleine went outside to meet Ryan, but as she did, she found her way blocked by Dominic. He was standing astride the walkway, blatantly barring her way.

"Please Dominic," she asked, "Let me pass. I have to meet my husband."

"Mm," he responded silkily, "I rather like the sound of that. Say 'please Dominic' again. I could serve you better than a boy from the bogland. A woman like you needs a grown man."

"Don't be foolish Dominic, you're my cousin."

"Only by marriage. Besides, cousins should show each other affection, don't you agree?" he responded.

His look put her in mind of a reptile, and he grew bolder, laying his hands on her shoulders, like a slimy toad. She felt only disgust towards him, and pulled away, turning to go back and escape from him. But Edward was waiting at the corner. Dominic turned her back to face him, and putting one hand firmly on her breast, and the other at the back of her neck, he drew her roughly against him.

She'd seen, but he hadn't, that Ryan was coming up quickly behind him. She'd never seen Ryan lose his temper so explosively before and it almost frightened her. Almost faster than her eyes could follow, he spun Dominic around, threw him bodily against the wall, pinned him there with his fists against her cousin's throat, and then he drew one hand back to punch him. The primeval rage Ryan was displaying made Madeleine hesitate to touch him, but she grasped his clenched fist and begged him to stop, knowing that violence was exactly what Margaret was hoping for. She was amazed and pleased that at her touch he was tamed instantly. He looked down at her, anger still in his eyes momentarily, and then they softened.

He turned briefly back to Dominic, and said fiercely, "Be sure you never lay hands on her again!" And then, with a contemptuous shove, Ryan pushed him aside, put his arm around his wife, and led her away. Edward had hidden himself from them, and when they reached the corner, both cousins attacked at the same time. Dominic crashed into Ryan from behind, sending Madeleine reeling too, and pushed him into Edward, and all three men ended up on the ground. As they scrambled to their feet, Edward got a grip on Ryan from behind, and Dominic took his opportunity to punch him forcefully in the ribs, causing him to double over, gasping for breath.

"Come, come!" Dominic leaned down and yelled in Ryan's face, "Let's see if you have the balls of a man, enough to keep our cousin at home!"

Ryan exploded into aggression and lunged forwards, his head hitting Dominic squarely on the nose, making blood spurt from it. Ryan's weight and momentum dragged Edward around, and he crashed into the wall, banging his head. It all happened so quickly, that before Madeleine knew it, Ryan had helped her to her feet and led her back inside, leaving the cousins reeling, bleeding, and cursing him.

As they were lying together that night Madeleine couldn't help but smile. She couldn't imagine any other man making her feel the way Ryan did. He needed no lessons from anyone in the art of pleasuring a woman.

The next day was 4th December, and there was snow. It was a day they would always remember because a strange bright star was seen in the sky, apparently passing into and then out of, the sun. People thought it was a bad omen, and Madeleine was filled with dread by it. The snow covered the ground more deeply than they'd ever seen before. Ryan would not let Madeleine be glum, or afraid of the omen, telling her that the star was like their love, and would survive anything, even the heat of the sun. He chivvied her along until she caught his mood and the two of them started playing in the snow like excited children, throwing snowballs at each other. She was better at it than Ryan. His throws were more forceful and hit harder, but hers hit their target more often, and so Ryan was soon covered in snow. He ran at Madeleine in mock fury, and tumbled her into a snow bank. Then he pushed handfuls of the icy snow down the neck of her gown, while she squealed and struggled. Eventually, when he felt she'd paid enough, he let her up. She was still giggling, but shaking with cold, so he took off his coat and wrapped it around her. The snowflakes drifted down from a darkening sky, covering his hair and melting into the cotton of his shirt as he stood in the snow, smiling at her. Then he put her across his shoulder, and carried her into the kitchen, still laughing and shivering equally.

Nancy stared at them in astonishment, and then as Ryan put Madeleine down, she started to fuss over them, pulling them both over to the fire. She brought hot spiced wine to them, and soon they were warm, their faces glowing in the firelight. Madeleine could feel her cheeks burning as the sensation returned to them. Ryan's face was ruddy with the light from the flames, and the heat from the snow. His eyes were so alive, so blue, his dark hair accentuating them that she thought they matched the colour of a peacock's breast.

By February 1640, things only got worse, as Margaret became ever more inventive.

One bedtime, Madeleine was summoned to the drawing room, and Ryan waited anxiously for her return, listening closely for any sound of trouble. By the time she returned she seemed tired and uncommunicative. Ryan had been in bed by then and he drew her in beside him, skin against skin. She didn't want to talk, only to sleep. He cradled her to him comfortingly.

The next morning all seemed normal. Early in the day Ryan and Nancy were sent to the mill in the pony and trap, on a regular errand. But when they returned in the afternoon, several armed men greeted them at the gate. Nancy was allowed to continue inside, but Ryan was forced at sword point to get down from the cart, and he wasn't permitted any further.

Nancy was very upset and protested, but there wasn't anything she could do, only call out to Ryan, "Don't leave! Wait for me!"

Leave? That was the last thing he was thinking of. He didn't know *what* to do though. His mind reeled in confusion, screaming out, wanting to know what was happening. But he had no one to turn to. He sat down at the side of the gate, despite the threats of the armed men, and made it plain by his demeanour that he wasn't leaving.

Finally, as darkness began to creep across the landscape, inky shadows running before it, Madeleine's mother and father walked haughtily down to him. It was getting very cold and Ryan stood up stiffly. Madeleine's father tossed a pouch of coins at him. He made no move to catch it and the bag bounced off his chest, and fell to the ground.

"Your bribery won't work now," he said, perplexed, "as it didn't work before."

"This isn't a bribe," her father told him, "It's more…compensation. Madeleine has finally seen the error of marrying below her station. She's locked herself in her bedroom, and she won't leave it until you've left the county."

"No," Ryan said, no doubt in his voice. "What you say is impossible."

"Are you so vain?" Margaret scorned. "Didn't you realise this would happen sooner or later? Your boorish ways were bound to offend her in the end. What do you think we were discussing with her last evening?"

Ryan couldn't answer for he didn't know, but he had an unshakeable belief that they were lying. Madeleine simply wouldn't and couldn't, do that to him.

"I'll tell you," Margaret continued, smiling, for she realised that he didn't know what they'd discussed. "She told us that she'd tired of your common ways. But she was afraid to tell you herself; for fear that you would strike out at her as you have at others when they've angered you."

Ryan's eyes narrowed. He hadn't doubted Madeleine but, even if he had, that statement proved they were lying.

So now he could answer, "You tell a poor lie. Madeleine knows one thing above anything else. She knows I'd never hurt her. You've tried to be too clever, and your plot has foundered."

"Believe what you will. Madeleine won't see you again. She won't leave the house, and if you're wise, you won't try to enter it." With this, Edwin turned to the armed men. "See to it that he leaves.

If necessary, run him through!'"

Ryan turned away from the gate in disgust, leaving the money pouch where it had fallen. He looked back over his shoulder to see Margaret stoop to retrieve it, and then he went into the woodland. Once he was out of sight and could no longer feel their cold gaze between his shoulder blades, he climbed up into a tree to think. He knew they were lying about Madeleine being in the house. If she was, then she'd never have allowed this to happen. He sighed heavily. If he knew what he had to do to win Margaret and Edwin over, then he'd do it. But it had gone too far. Margaret's hatred of him was obsessive. He shivered, both with the chill in the air and the ice of Margaret's hatred.

He knew another thing for sure; he wasn't going to leave, nothing would make him do that. With Madeleine he had found a life, and love. It was hard, very hard at times, to withstand the constant bombardment of hatred that was directed at him but his life without her now would be meaningless. Whenever the two of them were together it made up for all the tough times. She healed him and he knew she felt the same.

He slid down from the tree and made his way through the woods, so that he'd be able to see the main gate and yet remain unobserved. He put a hand to his stomach to stifle the sound as it rumbled loudly; he was hungry, but that would have to wait. He was also freezing cold and he knew that a night outdoors could well kill him. Darkness overtook the land, yet there was a bright full moon flooding the earth with her white power. Madeleine didn't come home that evening. He grew very concerned. Where was she? He wouldn't even consider that her parents were telling the truth. Madeleine loved him with her whole being and she'd never be parted from him voluntarily. That spawned his real worry, because she must therefore surely be held somewhere, a hidden prisoner. He hated not knowing where she was.

Finally, he had no choice but to retreat to a nearby barn, to huddle in the hay among some cattle, which at least kept him from freezing to death. He spent a fairly uncomfortable night, growing hunger adding to his woes. He'd been able to drink from the brook so he thanked God that at least thirst wasn't a problem. Thankfully also, Nancy didn't let him down. The first tendrils of early morning light had barely begun to creep against his eyelids when he heard her calling out to him. He responded, rubbing sleep from his eyes.

"Nancy? I'm here," he called, coming out of the barn.

She appeared through the trees and he ran to her, knowing that he'd find comfort there. He hugged her in appreciation of her loyalty and she hugged him in return.

"Thank the Lord," she breathed fervently. "Madeleine would never have forgiven me if you'd been driven off. "Here..." she handed him a cloth containing bread and cheese.

"Nancy, you're a true and treasured friend, thank you. But, have you seen her? Do you know where she is?" Ryan asked, hoping against hope that she could give him a positive answer.

"All I know is that she's not in the house," Nancy responded, disappointingly. She placed a consoling hand on his arm, "Ryan, I wish I could tell you more. But I can only tell you that Madeleine loves you, and she can't be a party to what's happened."

"Thank you Nancy, but that's something I don't fear. I just ..." he paused, suddenly finding it hard to speak. "I can't stand not knowing where she is!"

After that early morning meeting, Ryan had searched all the

buildings on the estate, and the neighbouring ones, convinced that Madeleine must be a prisoner. But he found no trace. He was exhausted. She wasn't in the near vicinity; he was sure of that. They must have taken her miles away. How would he ever find her? He contemplated storming the house, and forcing them to tell him the truth. He'd seen that her parents had removed the armed guards, just because he had disappeared from their immediate sight. It seemed they really believed he'd gone. That stunned him. Did they really think his love was so shallow?

His hands and arms had been scratched and torn by brambles, from when he had searched the remote overgrown reaches of the farm, disused barns that could have held a secret prisoner. He was dirty and tired. His limbs ached from the ground he had covered, but most of all it was his heart that ached.

Two hours later he walked along the main road. Some unknown force he'd been too tired to resist had drawn him there. When the carriage appeared, he'd thought he must be dreaming. For seated up next to the driver, was Madeleine. She cried out when she saw him, obviously delighted at the unexpected rendezvous. Ryan's energy reappeared, as if by magic, and he ran towards the carriage, his heart thumping in his chest.

The carriage pulled up sharply, the driver having no choice, for Ryan all but dived under the horses' hooves. Madeleine half-climbed and half-fell from the tall seat, anxiety etched on her face. Ryan caught her, lifted her, and spun her around, before setting her back on her feet and kissing her soundly, his eyes glistening with released joy.

"What is it? What is it?" she gasped, breathless from the kiss.

Ryan was almost speechless, but he managed to ask, "Where

have you been?"

"Didn't you get my note?" she asked puzzled, "I left it for you in our bedroom."

"I've not been allowed access to the house, or even the grounds, since my return from the mill."

"You've what? Oh...God!" She understood, and she tightened her embrace, "I've only been at my aunt's. She was dying and she asked for me to attend her."

"Your parents told me that you were in the house but that you'd tired of me. That you were afraid to face me, for fear that I'd hurt you."

"You didn't...?' she broke in, but Ryan held up a hand in denial.

"No. Of course I didn't believe them. But..." He stopped for a moment, staring intently at her face, and then he closed his eyes and sighed, the tension only now beginning to release him. "...I didn't know where you'd gone. I've been searching, searching every place I could think of. I feared you were a prisoner and I couldn't find you!"

This last sentence exploded from him on a sobbing breath of emotion. She stared at him. His eyes were bruised from lack of sleep, his was mouth drawn with worry; his clothes were stained and ragged, and there was blood on his hands and arms.

"My God," she said. "Oh Ryan..." She hugged him wordlessly.

After a while they both climbed into the carriage. Madeleine wanted to confront her parents, to rail and scream at them for their cruel behaviour. But Ryan persuaded her that the best way to make Margaret and Edwin understand that they were wrong, and had failed, was for the two of them to return home together, reunited as if nothing had happened. As they rode, Madeleine solved the rest of the mystery for him. When she'd been summoned to the drawing room the night before she disappeared, it was merely to face one more set of demands to admit that their marriage had been a mistake, which of course she had refused to do. The verbal attack on her and Ryan had left her weary, and she'd seen no point in troubling him with an account of it. The call to her ailing aunt the next morning had just been an opportune coincidence, which her parents had taken full advantage of.

Ryan had been right in that they should quietly return home together. Margaret's face when they strolled in, arm in arm was sweet revenge. She was incandescent with fury that her plan had failed, but also pale with defeat. Madeleine thanked God for Nancy. Thanked God that someone took care of Ryan for her.

CHAPTER TWENTY

There was one frightening time in early March of that year, when Ryan was able to repay Nancy for all her kindness to him. He and Madeleine had been out for an early evening stroll and were returning home by the longer route, using the lane. They heard the sound of a pony and trap coming very fast, and they stopped and waited to see who it was. When it hove into view they saw that it was Nancy who held the reins, and that she was driving the pony on with a whip. When she saw Ryan and Madeleine standing at the side of the road, Nancy pulled the pony to a sudden halt and climbed down to them, shaking from head to foot.

"Nancy, whatever's wrong?" Madeleine asked.

Nancy took a faltering step towards Ryan, and sensing her need, he put his arms around her. "It's all right Nancy," he said soothingly.

She started to cry, and Madeleine joined in with the hug. After a few moments, Nancy was calmer, "Oh dear," she said, "such a dreadful business...two men, villains and blackguards! They stopped the pony and demanded money or jewellery from me to let me pass. As if I look like a fine lady!"

"What did they do to you?" Ryan asked anxiously.

"They just frightened me half to death with vile threats and unseemly suggestions. I managed to drive the pony on through them. They chased me down the lane. Lord save us, they had knives!" She shuddered in remembered fear.

Ryan tried to reassure her. "It's all right now. Get back into the trap. You too, Madeleine. There isn't room for three, so I'll follow on foot, in case they're still coming after you."

"No!" Madeleine exclaimed. She wouldn't hear of it. She wasn't going to leave Ryan to the mercy of two armed men, even if the trap wasn't meant to hold three. "You'll ride with us, Ryan, or I won't leave."

Ryan rode standing on the back step of the trap, clinging to the rail, while Nancy and Madeleine rode inside. As it turned out it was fortunate for all of them that Madeleine had insisted Ryan ride with them, because the two robbers turned out to be very determined. The three of them had been travelling for only a few minutes in the trap, when the same two men came out of the woods just ahead of them and jumped down into the lane. They must have cut through the woods in order to catch up with the trap. Nancy tried to drive the pony through them again but they'd anticipated it this time and were carrying large branches, which they used to hit the pony about the head.

Nancy tried to contain the frightened animal, but he plunged from the road, rearing up at the bank, trying to climb it. Before anyone could do anything, he'd dragged the trap sideways up it. Then, still panicking, he galloped into the trees. They were nearly all thrown off at that point, especially Ryan who clung to the back. But, after a few hundred feet, one wheel of the trap hit a tree and broke. All the passengers were thrown out, and the terrified pony turned for home, dragging the wrecked trap behind him.

Madeleine rolled over and over, crashing through the undergrowth, thinking she'd never stop, but finally she did, lying breathless there for a moment. When she sat up she could see that Ryan and Nancy were alright. Ryan hurried over to her, and then to Nancy, to make sure they weren't hurt. Fortunately they'd landed in thick grass, which had cushioned their fall. Once they were all on their feet, they started to make their way back to the lane. But then they could hear the two men ahead of them, coming their way. Still they wouldn't give up! They were making no attempt to move quietly, and were obviously very confident. The trio backtracked quickly into the deeper woodland for they knew the men were armed with knives. There were very few places to hide as the trees were bare of leaves and their skeleton branches gave no cover at all. Luckily they came across a dense thicket of holly, covered with ivy, and crawled inside to hide. It wouldn't save them for long because it was an obvious hiding place, but it gave them a chance to think.

Nancy was terrified and she began to wail, "Lord save us! We'll be butchered!" She couldn't help herself, but she had to stop or she would have given their position away.

Ryan placed a hand on each of her cheeks and turned her face until her eyes met his. "Listen to me, Nancy," he pleaded with her, "I swear I won't let them harm you! Nancy! Do you trust me? Do you?"

"Yes," she answered tearfully.

He held her gaze, and repeated, "I won't let them harm you. I'll die first, do you hear me?"

"Yes," she responded again but in a steadier voice this time.

The men were almost upon them. Madeleine cast about in her mind for a plan, since it was obvious that they'd be found in the end, and she didn't want Ryan to try and tackle two armed men.

He spoke again, "You must both trust me. I want you to step out of hiding, right away, before they find us at this disadvantage. Pretend you're alone but remember, you are *not,* and remember that I won't let them hurt you."

Madeleine looked into his eyes and although she was deathly afraid of confronting the men, she did trust Ryan with her life. But she was also afraid for him. There being no time to argue or discuss, she grasped Nancy's hand and pulled her out into the open. They didn't need to pretend to be scared, and they clung to each other. Madeleine stifled a scream as the two men ran out of the trees. At the sight of the two women, they slid to a halt.

"Well, well now," one said, "What do we have here? Ladies, don't you know it's foolish to venture into these woods so late in the day?" The men didn't seem to think they were in any danger, and their knives at that point were sheathed in their belts. Madeleine started to hope that they'd not in fact seen Ryan, crouched as he'd been at the back of the trap, and that they thought the two women to be alone.

"You're fortunate it's us who have come across you, not some cut-throat robbers." The man grinned, showing grimy, yellow teeth. He leered at his companion, and as their eyes met, there were no special powers needed to guess their intentions.

"We'll see you safe home, never fear," said the other man, "After we've extracted a small payment." He too grinned in a revolting manner. "Come here!" he ordered, beckoning to Madeleine. She didn't move.

"I have nothing to pay you with," she replied.

"Oh, but you have, you have," he responded and, to her terror, he drew his blade, shouting at her, "Come here, now!"

Still she didn't move.

The other man also pulled his knife, "Cut her!" he said. "Her appreciation of you will improve."

Madeleine's heart thudded painfully in fear, *My God*, she

thought, *he'll really use the knife on me.*

At that moment, to her surprise and relief, for she'd seen no sign of his approach, Ryan suddenly stepped from behind a tree at the men's backs. He swung a hefty branch through the air, aimed at the head of one of the would-be attackers. Madeleine didn't know whether it was her or Nancy who gave him away with a look of relief, but one of them did. The man spun round to face Ryan. The blow still landed and its power was still enough to fell the man, but didn't knock him senseless, as it otherwise would have done. Ryan quickly struck again. This time the job was completed but the branch had broken, and the second man was now warned.

As the second blow had fallen on his companion, he had glanced at Nancy and Madeleine, and knife in hand he took a step towards the women, his intentions clear.

Ryan jumped over the unconscious body and quickly put himself between the other man and his intended victims. The man advanced on him, his blade flashing from hand to hand as he sought an opening. Then he struck, the blade arching through the air inches from Ryan's chest as he stepped back to avoid it. In a moment of premonition Madeleine could already imagine his blood spilling red against his white shirt, and she whimpered in terror. Twice more the blade slashed through the air, and Ryan barely avoided it. Now he could retreat no more, for Nancy and Madeleine were close behind him, while behind them was an impenetrable tangle of bushes. Madeleine's hands were against Ryan's back and there was nowhere left for them to go. Time seemed to slow down. She could feel Ryan's muscles through the rough fabric of his shirt, stretching and contracting as he drew back from the knife. She could feel his heart pounding with intense effort. And in her mind's eye she could see him falling in front of her.

Then suddenly it was over. Ryan saw the chance he'd obviously been waiting for and grabbed at the man's knife. Immediately blood welled from Ryan's clenched fist, and Madeleine could see that his hand hadn't caught just the man's hand and the hilt, but also part of the blade itself. The robber twisted the knife but Ryan wouldn't let go. With his other hand he managed to hit the man in the ribs. The man fell and Ryan was able to wrest the knife from him. The man gasped for breath, and Ryan quickly turned the knife and hit him hard on the temple with the heavy hilt.

Once they were safe, Ryan clasped his injured hand and flinched at the pain of the cut. Nancy and Madeleine both took hold of his arm anxiously, and made him open the hand for them to see the extent of the wound. His palm was sliced across from one side to the other, but the blade must have turned because fortunately it had cut broadly but not deeply. Nancy strode over to one of the fallen robbers, fearless by then, and tore off a length of his shirt. This they used to bind Ryan's hand and staunch the bleeding. Then both women hugged him in thanks for saving them.

CHAPTER
TWENTY-ONE

In April 1640, Margaret decided to hold one of her dinner parties. She was just amusing herself, and at the same time, if arranged carefully, it would provide her with a useful tool in her attempts to put a wedge between Ryan and Madeleine. She knew how excited Madeleine used to be when she was welcomed at that kind of party. Margaret couched her invitation carefully, giving Madeleine the impression that both she *and* her husband were included, for she knew her stepdaughter would never have agreed to come without him.

As she had hoped, Madeleine fell for the ruse, and did get very excited at the prospect of dressing up in her finery, even more so because she thought Ryan would be there too. She told Ryan in their bedroom, and was disappointed when he frowned and said that he did not want to go.

"But why?" she asked. "After all this time, you've been included. Isn't that what we wanted, that she would eventually accept you?"

"Did she actually use those words? That you *and* your husband were to come?"

"Well, no," Madeleine so wanted to believe it was true, "but I'm sure that's what she implied, she certainly didn't say you *weren't* invited, and surely she *must* know that I wouldn't go without you, so why invite me, without you?"

"That's true," he thought about it for a few moments, "If it makes you happy I'll come, but don't be surprised if it turns out to be another of her tricks. I don't believe she will ever accept me."

When the day of the party came, Madeleine dressed up in her best silk gown, with ribbons and pearls in here hair. She looked very beautiful, and Ryan told her so. He put on the dark blue, silky shirt that Nancy had made him and his best black breeches. Madeleine brushed his hair and then combed it neatly back into the fashion of the day, a side-tail, like a pony tail but pulled over to one side, rather than dangling straight down his back. Ryan seemed uneasy, but Madeleine knew that was only natural. He didn't like rubbing shoulders with the gentry at the best of times, and he would still be thinking this was a trick. Madeleine didn't think so, because since the invitation Margaret had discussed the menu with her, and had even asked, "What does your like to husband eat?" So, Madeleine was convinced that Ryan was expected.

At 6.30pm Ryan followed his wife downstairs and they both went into the dining room. Two swordsmen were standing at either side of the double doors, and it was obvious immediately that Ryan had been right all along. As the men stepped forwards, swords drawn, and got between her and Ryan, Madeleine gasped in disbelief and horror. Margaret was standing at the head of the table, a smirk on her face.

"Oh there you are, Madeleine, dear," she said, "But you seem to have an undesirable attached to you. Gatecrashers are so boring. Take him out!"

Madeleine turned to follow, as Ryan was bustled back through the door.

"Oh no my dear, I have several young men coming tonight who are very keen to meet you."

"Are you insane?" Madeleine asked, perplexed, still trying to follow Ryan, but being blocked by the two swordsmen, "I have no wish to meet any of your 'young men'. Get out of my way!" she yelled at the two men.

"Madeleine!" Margaret stopped her, "We don't want anyone to get hurt, now do we? I think you'd better come and sit down, before the gatecrasher is accidentally run through."

Still Madeleine tried to follow her husband, but they wouldn't let her through. She could see the point of one sword pricking Ryan's neck, so she stopped, frustrated.

He called out to her, "It doesn't matter. It's just a dinner party. I'll wait for you upstairs."

"You see," gloated Margaret, "he knows his place better than you do. Now, sit down! Or I'll have to give an order you will not like!"

Madeleine walked angrily to the chairs, and dragging one squealing across the floor, she sat down on it, a glower on her face.

Soon, other guests started to arrive, and Madeleine was forced to make small talk with them, scowling all the while. Two eligible young men had been invited and they tried to engage her, as they had obviously been coached to do. Madeleine almost spat in their faces. Her attitude, obvious to everyone, drew the attention of Louise Capjohn, one of Margaret's friends.

She asked her hostess, "Whatever is wrong with your step-daughter? She looks as if she has swallowed a wasp."

Margaret raised her voice deliberately, "My dear, she has married a peasant, without our permission, and now regrets it."

Louise gasped in delighted shock, and turned to Madeleine, "You poor thing. Can you not get rid of him?"

"I do not wish to get rid of him," Madeleine retorted, "I love him.

My stepmother is jealous."

Louise gasped ecstatically, turning back to Margaret, "Really? Are you? Is he handsome?"

Margaret laughed, "The poor girl is embarrassed to have only managed to snare an Irish gypsy as a husband. He is boorish, bad-mannered, and the produce of a slut!"

"But is he *handsome*?" Louise insisted, smiling.

"What do one's looks matter, if one has no breeding?" Margaret answered.

"True, but if he's handsome he might have his uses."

"He is of no use for anything at all. That I can swear to. His lack of breeding shows in everything he does. My dear you should see how he dresses!" She pretended to lower her voice to a conspiratorial whisper, but kept it loud enough so that everyone could hear, "He looks as if he was given birth to in a thruppenny brothel!"

Louise laughed, and so did everyone else at the table.

Madeleine couldn't help it, her anger took over, and she said, "My husband is of blue blood! Should he wish it, he could claim the Earldom of Kildare!"

Silence fell, seconds ticked by, and then Margaret started to laugh. Soon everyone, except Madeleine joined in, as the succulent morsel of gossip was passed around the table.

Margaret finally contained herself, "Oh you silly, silly girl, you would believe anything he told you, wouldn't you."

"It is true," Madeleine insisted, but quietly, as she was already regretting her outburst. She pushed back her chair, got up and left the room, but not before she caught Margaret's speculative look. *Oh my God,* she thought, *what have I done?* Margaret was a lot of things, but she was not stupid. She just might figure it out. Madeleine rushed to the bedroom and confessed all to Ryan.

He reassured her, "Don't worry, she won't remember it by morning. She's probably drunk two bottles of wine already."

But Madeleine felt a dark cloud gathering.

Madeleine was right in as much as Margaret didn't forget the odd conversation. She and Edwin talked about it at lot, trying to understand why Madeleine had said it. Margaret sensed that it was something that could be used against Ryan, if she could only figure out how. If there was any truth in it, then why wouldn't the Irishman have come to the house all puffed up with his own importance? If he'd done that he might have been able to marry Madeleine with their blessing. It couldn't be true, and yet, though Margaret hated to admit it, there was *something* about him that set him aside from the other peasants. He had a certain bearing and a certain temperament. Of course it was smothered beneath his rough exterior, but it was there. And that gold ring he wore, where had that come from? If it was true....finally Margaret realised, Madeleine had said, 'He could claim', not 'He is the Earl', Of course, it must be a contested title! There must be another contender for the title in Ireland, probably a member of the family. Suddenly she had it. He was illegitimate - how *obvious* now that she knew! A bastard by birth, but with some sort of claim! That meant that just possibly, over in Ireland, there was someone who wanted Fitzgerald dead as much as she did!

Margaret's husband had good political connections, and so she got names and addresses and sent out letters to Ireland by courier, to see if her fishing could create a trap that would get rid of the interloper for her. In the meantime she would carry on with her other plan to get rid of him herself.

CHAPTER TWENTY-TWO

One day, just two weeks before Margaret finally got her evil way, and Ryan was lost to Madeleine for good, something happened that made her actions more desperate and determined than ever. That day probably sealed his fate more than any other.

On 6th May 1640, Margaret held a garden party. Ryan and Madeleine were instructed to keep well out of the way as usual. Margaret liked to use these occasions to make fools of people. Madeleine supposed her stepmother gained a perverse kind of power from it. She had a really cruel streak in her, which enjoyed anyone else's misery. She'd often invite one or two totally unsuitable couples to her parties, fostering their belief that they'd been accepted into the higher echelons of society, but in reality they were there for the sole purpose of amusing her other guests. Their clothes of course would always generate ridicule.

On this particular day even that wasn't enough for her. She'd hatched a really evil plot with some of her cronies. A well-meaning, kindly couple called John and Monica Barrett arrived at the party, their faces shining with pride at being welcomed in high society. They found to their amazement that they were apparently fully accepted by everyone, and they seemed to be meriting a flattering amount of attention from the other guests.

After an hour or so, Margaret's plan was put into action. With a gesture, she got them to turn around so that they were suddenly confronted by a very regal-looking man and woman, who were dressed in fine silks and velvets. The man regarded the Barretts with disdainful expectation, staring down his nose at them. Neither poor John nor his wife knew what was expected of them and they stood unmoving, in total bewilderment. The foppish man was holding a lace handkerchief, which he flicked from side to side as if in impatience. John and Monica could hear the crowd around them beginning to mutter and snigger but they had no idea what they were supposed to do.

"M…my Lord?" John finally stammered, inquiringly.

At this the man spoke angrily: "Do you not bow before your sovereign?" he demanded.

"M…my God, the K…king!" John stuttered, "Your Highness! I beg your forgiveness! I'm so sorry!"

The poor pair fell to their knees in mortification, their faces reddening. At this, the entire assemblage, including the 'king', who was of course not the king at all, broke into uproarious laughter. It took several moments before the Barretts realised that they'd been made into complete fools.

Margaret completed their discomfort by saying loudly, "Now perhaps you'll have learned not to try and stand amongst those who are your superiors! From now on, stay with the common peasants where you belong!"

The whole company laughed again, and John and Monica could only flee in abject shame. In their hurry to escape the garden they took a wrong turn and collided with Nancy at the kitchen door. By this time Monica was in tears and her husband was near to it.

"My dears, my dears!" exclaimed Nancy. "Whatever's wrong?" They were incapable of speaking clearly, so Nancy ushered them into the kitchen, her safe haven for all.

Ryan and Madeleine were seated at the table, keeping out of Margaret's way. After a while, when the Barretts could speak again, the whole sorry tale was recounted. As always when he was roused, either with pleasure or in anger, Ryan's eyes darkened in colour and started to glint dangerously. He was very tolerant and would normally endure a lot of goading, but the cruel antics of some rich folk annoyed him to the point where he had to act. He stood up hurriedly, pushing his chair back with an aggressive shove, and strode out of the back door without a word. Nancy and Madeleine looked at each other, no words necessary between them. They both knew that when Ryan was like that there was no stopping him. He had a reckless heart.

They all watched and listened from the back doorway. Margaret didn't notice Ryan at first, but gradually she realised that silence was descending over her yet mirthful guests as he pushed his way none too gently between them in order to reach her.

Seeing him pushing between her silk-clad guests in his rough clothes, she screeched, "How dare you! Get back to the servants' quarters where you belong! You'll regret this!" Perhaps she sensed that he was about to get his revenge for her humiliation of Madeleine at the dinner party, in front of all Margaret's high-class friends.

Ryan stood and looked around at the gathered guests, very out of place among all the strutting 'peacocks' that adorned the gardens.

He interrupted her before she could continue, "Ladies and gentlemen, it's my misfortune to have cause to call this lady, my mother-in-law." He paused as gasps of amazement and glee could be heard all around, as the crowd sensed blood, "And how dare *you* treat decent people in this appalling way? They've done you no harm although, as I well know, that's not necessary in order to fall foul of

your despicable mind. The Barretts may not be able to call themselves members of your high society, but they are more deserving of
being called members of the human race than all of you are."

Margaret was flustered, and her only answer was to hit out. So
she tried to slap Ryan in the face as she'd once done before, but he
caught her wrist and held it tightly.

"No," he said, "not again."

She struggled but he wouldn't let her loose. "Let me go!" she
screamed, looking around her for support.

But like a pack of jackals, her friends soon turned on their own in
times of trouble. Besides, there wasn't anyone there man enough to
try and tackle Ryan in his angry mood. When he'd held her wrist
long enough for her to understand that she'd get no help from her
friends, and that he had power over her, he let her go with a quick
disdainful flick and turned to walk back to the kitchen.

That might have been the end of it, except that right in his path,
standing next to the ornamental pond and fountain, was the man
who'd played the part of the king. It was obvious that Ryan couldn't
resist. As he came abreast of the man he turned and bowed in
mock humility.

"Your Majesty!" he said, and in one swift movement he barrelled
into the 'king' at waist height, and tossed him over the wall and into
the pond. With a startled shriek the pretender floundered on his back
in the water in complete panic. Without a backward glance, Ryan
returned to the group at the back door.

Now it was John and Monica's turn to laugh, and Madeleine laughed
too. But underneath she was concerned. Ryan did himself no good at all
by antagonising Margaret. But he was only being himself and, as she
loved him to his very soul, she wouldn't have had him any other way.

CHAPTER TWENTY-THREE

Finally, Margaret had realised that the only way to be rid of Ryan was to arrange to have him taken away and killed. That way she would avoid having his blood directly on her hands, and yet be certain that he could never return. She had not had a reply from Ireland, and she could bear to wait no longer. She would have him taken to a place he could never return from, and a place where death was almost a certainty.

It was a beautiful day, 20th May 1640. Ryan and Madeleine were walking through the gardens and into the woods beyond. Ryan was carrying a hawk that had been injured some weeks previously, and was ready for release. It was still early, and the trees ahead of them were swathed in a ground mist so that it appeared as if they were about to wade through a waist-high sea. As the sun rose it filtered through the trees, glinting on each droplet of water that dangled from the leaves, turning each one into a bright crystal of fire and ice. As they walked across lawns of the garden, their passage created an emerald trail through the gossamer cobwebs that were strung across the grass. The trees, wreathed in skeins of ever shifting mist, stood in silent communion with each other.

The darting movements of a deer caused the hawk's head to bob with interest, its eyes glittering. Ryan looked at the bird, and their eyes met in apparent genuine communication. When they reached a small clearing, Ryan released the hawk, and it lit on a branch, watching them. Ryan pushed Madeleine gently backwards against a tree trunk. She could feel its passive strength at her back. He pinned her to the tree with his own body weight, and smiled down at her. He clasped both her hands in his, twining their fingers together, then stretched her arms out to the sides, and, leaning in, he kissed her. Madeleine could feel his passion growing against her skirt, and, illogically shy under the steady gaze of the hawk she broke away from him and ran through the trees, laughing. Ryan chased her and caught her easily as they cleared the trees, and he pulled her down in the long grass of the meadow. He was persuasive as always; the touch of his hands drawing an answering heat from Madeleine, despite the chilliness of the early morning air and the dampness of the dew. Time passed unnoticed by either of them...

Their clothes were dishevelled and Madeleine's hair was loose. As they rested there in each other's arms she could see the hawk wheeling slowly overhead, a distant silhouette against the pure blue of the sky. Her modesty had been wasted after all.

Suddenly the mood was broken as they heard the sound of hunting horns coming from the house. Thinking that there must have been some dreadful disaster, they got up and started running home. Halfway there, Ryan suddenly stopped, and grasping Madeleine's arm, he brought her to a stop too. He didn't want to go back, and he told her that he sensed danger. There'd been talk of an impending war with Scotland, and they had both feared that her parents might use it as an excuse to have him sent away to join the army. Even though this was the English King's fight against the Scottish and Ryan was Irish, that wouldn't make him safe.

But Madeleine was sure that it would be all right. She was convinced that whatever plans Margaret might hatch that her father wouldn't betray his daughter. If there was some plot going on, then the two of them would leave, and never come back. Edwin would know that and he wouldn't want to lose his daughter.

They knew something bad was happening because they were summoned into the music room, and Ryan had never been allowed in there before. Margaret and Edwin told them both that the King was amassing an army to fight the Scottish; that men from the Royal House had arrived to take all the young men from the estate off to fight. They said that Ryan had to go, and go that very minute. He had been right to fear a conspiracy, but Madeleine hadn't expected such sudden and violent action. She couldn't believe it.

Madeleine turned to run, but some men had come into the room behind her and at a signal from Edwin, the three of them took hold of Ryan very roughly, two pinning his arms to his sides, and the third putting his arm around Ryan's throat from behind. These were not the King's men, and Madeleine was sure she recognised some of them. Margaret and Edwin grasped Madeleine's arms, but she struggled from their grip and clutched Ryan's hands, screaming at the men to let him go. They grabbed her again and started to prise her and her husband's fingers apart. Cold horror seized her heart.

She cried out in terror, "Ryan! No! Ryan!" He struggled, but he was pulled relentlessly backwards out into the hallway. His eyes met hers despairingly. Madeleine knew his last look would live with her forever, as his eyes burned an image into hers. The door slammed shut on the melee, and she could hear Ryan shouting, then the sounds of a fight, and the dreadful sounds of blows hitting flesh. The noise died away as she struggled more fiercely, almost getting free, but Edwin called out for help. Two more men came into the room in response to his shouts, and bundled her out into the hall, which by then was empty. She was dragged upstairs and locked in the small room at the front of the house.

The walls of the small room were bare plaster, the door solid oak, and the only window was a narrow glassed slit. In desperation she lifted a chair and smashed the glass. The gap created was too small to escape through, though she tried, cutting her hands in the process. She could see the grounds below, and she reached her arm out of the gap, crying out Ryan's name over and over again as he was thrown bodily into the back of a wooden cart. The cart was driven away, and as she lost sight of it, and Ryan, she collapsed to the floor, sobbing. Her world was gone. She was sure that she'd never see him again. Her whole life had been totally destroyed in the space of a few minutes. She sat with her silk skirt hunched around her, its pale blue marred by the scarlet threads of blood from her cut hands. She stared around stupidly, with eyes that felt as if they were made of marble.

It had all happened so fast. As she looked around the room, the full nightmare struck. The room had been thoroughly prepared for a prisoner, with food and water enough for days. It had all been a despicable, well-planned trick. Those men, they hadn't been from the King, they were the same thugs that had beaten Ryan in the lane. This 'conscription' had been carefully arranged. Her parents had finally succeeded in betraying them, as Ryan had always feared they would. She'd been a fool and this was her punishment.

The next few months passed in a haze of grief and frustration.

Once let out of the room, Madeleine soon snuck out of the house and begged a ride in a passing carriage. She managed to get to the docks at Southampton, going there because all she knew was that Ryan had been taken to a ship. When it rained, she spent some time huddled miserably under a handcart with a street waif for company. It was warm, or she could have died from exposure and lack of food and drink. She was very fortunate not to be attacked by some drunken rapist, although she was long past caring about what happened to her. Without Ryan her life was meaningless. Her body was only for his use, and without him she didn't care what happened to it.

In the daytime she roamed from ship to ship, a pathetic sight, with tangled dirty hair, wet, grubby clothes, and a deranged look on her face. She was taunted by crude remarks from the sailors, while she searched for a trace of Ryan. She knew in her heart that it was useless, right from the start. Eventually Edwin traced her journey and sent some men to fetch her back. At the house she sent out letters to everyone she could think of who might take pity on her, but the world was sealed against her.

CHAPTER TWENTY-FOUR

The colour leached out of Madeleine's world and everything was total desolation. She went for a ride on Ryan's favourite horse and galloped wildly and recklessly through the woods. Branches lashed at both horse and rider in the wind, and infected with the wildness she could sense in her rider, the mare released a frenzy of speed. When they came to the meadow, the meadow she and Ryan had lain together in, Madeleine reined the horse in sharply. She screamed and pleaded with the wind to take her spirit away and spread it into the sky, so that she would not have to feel anything any more.

Uselessly she cried out loud "Ryan!" Over and over, praying, begging, that somehow he would hear her and come back to her. But the wind snatched her voice away in shreds, and she was still there alone. Tears were no longer enough. The relentless pain was destroying her. She felt as if a living part of her had been cruelly wrenched from her body and it would never, never heal. She rode the horse back to the woods, at a walking pace, their energy spent.

When she reached the glade that held their special oak tree, she sat for a moment staring at the late bluebells that still survived in the shady depths. A wave of fresh torment battered her and she threw herself down from the back of the horse. She fell to the ground, grief, fear, and frustration, bringing her to her knees. Kneeling amid the faded blooms, she closed her eyes. Her mind tried to bring comfort by drawing her back into the precious past. As she opened her eyes, just for a moment, all around her there appeared a sea of newly sprung bluebells. And there was Ryan walking towards her, a smile on his face. He loved the bluebells because they were rampant and unstoppable, flowing like blue, indigo fire under the trees. As he came nearer, she was struck by the way his eyes reflected the blue power that was spread at his feet.

She was transported for a moment, but inevitably the vision dissolved, and she was back in a world that she had nothing but loathing for. A sob caught in her throat as she realised with horror that if she remained in the world, then next spring she would have to endure the bluebells alone. It would be unbearable; how could they still live if *he* didn't? She was trapped in the centre of an endless, raging storm, wind blowing through her heart, and she knew she would not survive it.

Back at the house, the servants, all except Nancy, became afraid of Madeleine as she roamed the house, raging against fate, talking to someone who wasn't there. She had a feral look about her, with her untamed hair and mad eyes. She didn't change her clothes or bathe unless she was forced too. Talk spread in the town that a crazy woman lived at the house, and children sometimes hid in the garden, having been dared by their peers to catch a glimpse of her. Nancy tried to comfort her, but there was no comfort in her arms. The arms Madeleine longed for would never return.

One day in early August 1640, a group of men rode up to the house. They were dressed in kilts and were well-armed. At the sound of their voices Madeleine was briefly drawn from her encroaching madness, because they spoke with the same pleasing lilt as Ryan did. She ran to them, her hands twisting together in anguish. When she tried to talk to the men, and ask if they knew where Ryan was, they laughed at her. The leader, who shared the same dark looks as Ryan, told her not to worry, that he would find him. Edwin pulled her away, tears in his eyes, strong enough to overcome her, because she was only skin and bone by then. He loved her, but he knew he had left it too late to save her. There was no going back. Margaret dealt with the Irishmen, answering their questions and handing them a piece of paper. They seemed pleased with it, and rode off at speed.

In her lucid moments Madeleine tormented herself that she should have heeded the warnings of which there were many. *Ryan knew!* He'd always known, but she hadn't listened. Guilt racked her, alongside her grief. By 30th August, she knew that he was never coming back to her, that he was gone from this world. She knew she would have been able to sense his presence, no matter how far away he was, but when she reached out with her soul, there was nothing. Cold, empty darkness where once there was a fiery spark. It tore her heart in two even to think of it, but she knew he was dead. She wasn't even allowed to wear black, because Margaret would rather she denied they had ever been married. Madeleine knew that her love was somewhere out in the dark; wet, cold, alone, and unbearably still. Her arms ached to hold him, her hands to touch him, her whole body yearned to lie against him, but she knew that she never would again.

Finally, madness overtook her completely. She drifted like a wraith through a fantasy world. People talked to her but she didn't hear them. Their voices spoke to her as though through a mist. She talked to Ryan at night, and sometimes she even heard him answer her. She found some of his hair entwined in her hairbrush, though she swore it wasn't there before. She wove the hair strands into a ring and wore it all the time. When she walked in the woods she often saw Ryan. He was always shadowy, partly hidden, and just out of reach. She tried to follow him. Sometimes she even saw him in the house.

One night she saw him climbing the stairs, and followed him. He was going up into the attic, and she followed him. She could see him through the window, on the roof, and climbed out of the window to him. She couldn't see him immediately but then she heard him calling her name. He was below, in the courtyard, holding up his arms to her. With no fear at all, she stepped off the roof. Seemingly in slow motion, she flew, down and down. Suddenly Ryan vanished, and she screamed as she plunged towards the unyielding ground. White light seared her brain.

Ryan had been taken by ship to an area near Beverley Gate at Kingston Upon Hull. This was a training camp for conscripted soldiers. They were crudely trained in the use of a heavy bladed, two-handed sword, and only the strongest survived. The weapons provided were deliberately chosen for their clumsiness, and were more suited to mounted soldiers. This was because the men, considered criminals, might be dangerous if they were well-armed. Training them as Musketeers was obviously also out of the question, lest they turn the long-distance weapons on their captors.

Once, Ryan had to watch, horrified, as a weaker man was brutally killed by his trainer because he would never 'make the grade' and would have slowed the soldiers down. Ryan tried to escape once, even though he knew it was useless. He was driven to it because he felt such an overwhelming need to be held in the arms of someone who loved him. He was caught almost immediately, and lashed as a punishment. He was told that even if he were to survive the camp, and the war, he would never be released, because his 'conscription' had been arranged that way.

His group were sent by ship to Sunderland, and marched to the river crossing at Newburn Ford, where it was rumoured the Scottish would try and invade. But by the time they got there on 29th August, the Scottish had already crossed, and the English had lost the battle and fled in disarray. Hours later, as they tried to get back to the ship, Ryan's group were attacked by a larger group of English rebel soldiers who had deserted the main army, and they were rendered virtually weapon-less by them. At the time of the attack, Ryan and the other prisoner-soldiers were still in chains and not able to fight well. After this minor skirmish, because the officers had been slain, they were unchained and given small round shields, with 'sword-breaker' spikes on the front.

The next day, on 30th August, Ryan's group were passing by Lumley Castle when a mass of well-armed, kilted men came at them from the trees. Ryan wanted to run because he had no weapon, only a shield. Many of the men had been wounded in the previous skirmish and they tried to get shelter in the Castle. Those safe inside didn't want to get involved and would not open the gates. Ryan and the other able-bodied men had no choice but to try and defend the wounded. It wasn't until the first attacker had knocked him to the ground, wounded, that Ryan recognised the man who was following behind his initial attacker. It was his Irish half-brother, Gerald Fitzgerald. Ryan had no idea how he had been traced to this remote field, but even in his distress and pain, he was sure Margaret must have had a hand in it.

When Gerald struck him with his sword, Ryan knew the time had come. The point of the blade glinted red in the sunlight, as it emerged through his back. His blood sprayed scarlet onto the vile green of the grass. Ryan didn't scream, but as the blow struck, he rolled onto his left side, curled around the hilt of the sword. Gerald leaned down and snatched the gold Fitzgerald ring from Ryan's left hand.

He hissed, "You stole *my* ring, and *my* father's name. *This* is mine!" He left the sword embedded in his brother, and ran on.

As Ryan lay dying, he thought he saw Madeleine bending over him. He reached out a blood-soaked hand and tried to grasp hers as she reached for him. But his hand gripped nothing, as their fingers passed through each other.

CHAPTER TWENTY-FIVE

S o, back in my current life, I knew the whole story. I knew why I had been so depressed, so grief-stricken, and why seeing Ryan brought back to life on the TV screen as Garth Brooks had cured it. That part of me that was still Madeleine had recognised him. My soul recognised his soul. It was a painful and tragic journey I had been on, but I was happy I knew it all. Now that I knew who I had been, I knew who I really was.

There are still some questions. Madeleine's maiden name for instance. For a long time I have called her family De Port. This name came not from my own subconscious, but from that of the person who was once Nancy. She may be right, but I am unable to confirm it. I suspect that Madeleine does not want to remember being a member of the family that destroyed her love and her life. Those people who never realised that though blood might be thicker than water, love *is* thicker than blood.

I started to learn more about spiritual stuff, because this experience had taught me that I'd been right all along. There *was* an ultimate purpose behind everything. We *did* move on after this life, and not just cease to exist. I learned that the feeling of something missing that so many of us have is real. There *is* something that we all came here to do, and remembering what it is leads us to real happiness.

Tony and I discussed it all endlessly.

"It's not finished yet though, is it?" he asked one evening.

"Sorry, no it isn't. If I can I have to meet Garth …for her. I think that she's somehow lost him, I don't mean like back then, but that somehow in the… spirit world, they never got back together. Now I need to put that right. I don't really understand…I think Margaret changed their fate somehow. They were meant to die together. I think he was meant to die by his brother's hand, but *with* Madeleine, at the house. Because Margaret was so nasty and impatient, she had him sent away. If she hadn't done that, then Gerald would have found him at the house, Madeleine would have tried to stop Gerald, and she and Ryan would have died in each other's arms." I thought for a minute. "We know that Ryan was pretty much resigned to dying young, one day. I think he was happy to stay at the house and have it happen there, but being taken away, leaving her alone…no."

"I don't understand what you can do though; you can't change what happened…"

It was still coming through to my subconscious as I answered him, "Maybe I can. Maybe somehow, and I don't know how yet, I can bring them back together."

"Garth's over there, in America, and you're over here, and you know you won't fly. How's it going to happen?"

Tony was right. I had always had a terrible phobia about flying. Just the thought of it would make me feel sick and wobbly.

"I don't know how, but I know I have to try… I feel very guilty too about how Madeleine blurted out who Ryan really was to Margaret, maybe, if she hadn't…"

"No, he would have died anyway. In fact that was leading him and Madeleine to the way they *should* have died. You just said that yourself. It was Margaret who made things go wrong."

"I suppose, but I'd like to get a sign of forgiveness from Garth, or Ryan. Maybe if we meet, his attitude will tell me if he still loved Madeleine when he died, or if he blamed her at that moment."

I abruptly changed the course of the conversation. "Tone, I want you to give up your job. Hand your notice in. Tomorrow."

Tony's face took up a comical battle between daring to believe he could shake off that horrible yoke he'd carried for so long, just like that, and incredulity that I could suggest something so stupid.

"Don't be daft, and do what?"

"Sell the farm."

"No, no, we took so long to get it! It was our dream."

"I know, but you made the dream happen, and we've had it, and now we don't need it any more. Other things are more important."

"Like what?"

"Like you." I cuddled up to him.

"What would I do? How would we live..?" His voice petered out on a note of hope tinged with doubt.

"We'd buy a smaller, cheaper place, with no land. You wouldn't have to have such a highly paid job; you could be...um...a postman! Or start your own business. We'd only need enough to live on."

"Oh yeah and who's going to pay the mortgage?"

"We won't need one. Trust me. I've got it all worked out, we'll be able to pay ours off and have enough for a nice place without one."

Well it turned out I was right. Tony, showing ultimate trust in me, went gleefully into work the following week and handed in his notice, which meant we had a month before he stopped being paid; a month before we had to have sold the farm; a month before we had to find somewhere else to live. Along with all the other changes, I had developed a big sense of adventure! The time scale didn't worry me at all. It's a funny thing, when you take the first step on a path that's right, the path you were always meant to tread, things start to fall into place with amazing ease.

During the hypnosis, I'd made contact with what I call my higher self, and I had a new and wonderful sense that everything was going to work out just fine. Sure enough, within two weeks the farm was sold. We found great homes for the pet sheep and horses; paid off the mortgage, and moved into rented accommodation for a few weeks. Six weeks later we'd moved into a sweet and roomy bungalow with a small garden and no mortgage on the other side of the country. Then Tony had time to look around and decide what he would enjoy doing. Things weren't easy as we hadn't reckoned on how difficult it would be for him to find a nice little job.

Some months later I found out that Garth was doing a concert in Ireland. I could manage to get there! Success! It was going to work! Then of course I found out that all the tickets were sold. Then almost at the last minute it seemed that fate stepped in. A friend of mine, Hannah Valise, knew someone who had a spare ticket. Her friend, Keith Powell, had bought tickets for himself, his wife and his son, and his son had decided he didn't want his, and so I was able to have it. It meant sharing a hotel room with Keith and his wife, complete strangers, but Tony insisted I should go, and I wasn't going to look a gift horse in the mouth.

Finally, after what seemed like years of waiting, the day of the concert in Dublin loomed. We made it to the hotel in Dublin with less than an hour in hand, and from there to the stadium. I was numb by then, in a kind of limbo, wanting to see Ryan, but afraid that seeing him as Garth in concert, wasn't after all going to be enough for Madeleine's spirit.

Finally Garth appeared and there he was, right in front of me, in front of her. But almost right away I realised that it wasn't going to be enough. I was right 'up in the God's', so far away from the stage. Worse yet, I could feel no trace of Ryan in him. It seemed as if the huge megastar persona of 'Garth Brooks' left no room for anyone else. But Ryan was very charismatic too, so I waited hopefully for him to appear. If only I'd known the layout of the stadium, maybe I could have brought a ticket for the standing area, which was far below me. As it was a sheer drop separated me from the stage and there was no way down, and no way to get any closer. This was as near as I was going to get, and that was the problem for Madeleine. She needed eye contact; she needed to touch his hand. I hadn't realised that before.

Half way through the concert, things changed for the better, and for the worse, depending on how you looked at it. He was singing *The Dance,* when something extraordinary happened. I'd always thought of this as Ryan's theme song, ever since I'd first heard it. He was definitely a man who lived in the moment, and tended to leave the future to take care of itself. Half-way through the song Garth stared right up towards me intently, and I stared back, unblinking. Despite the distance, I was transfixed. He walked forward a few steps onto a platform that reached into the audience, ignoring the grasping hands that reached for him, as the crowd got excited.

Even though he was so far away, something was passing between us. Then the people in the audience seemed to sense something magical taking place. Those nearest to me lowered their hands and fell silent. All I could hear were the words of *The Dance* spiralling up through the night air, crystalline in their clarity. And for that time, for me, Garth was Ryan. These words were coming direct from

Ryan. I didn't know how that could be; I just knew that it was true. Time seemed to stand still, but in another sense it flew by. I felt every word that he sang deep inside my soul.

Looking back on the dance we shared...I could have missed the pain, but I'd have had to miss the dance. I certainly believe that it was worth all the pain I went through, as Madeleine, to know Ryan – dance the dance. I wouldn't have missed knowing him for anything. And even if I'd known how it would end, it would still have been worth it.

As if God had flicked a switch, the sounds of the crowd filtered back into my hearing, which for a time had heard only his voice. The concert reappeared around me. I realised that there were silent tears streaming down my face. The rest of the concert was dream-like. I was in another world, another time. I was elated, but I was also heartbroken. For right then, I was in torment. To have the soul that Madeleine loved, so near, and yet for her to be unable to touch him, was like offering a crumb of bread to a starving man, almost worse than nothing. The pain of losing Ryan had been eased, but the pain of wanting to look into his eyes, up close, to hold him, remained deep in my soul – her soul. A union of some sort needed to take place, and it hadn't happened. I walked back to the hotel in a daze. All the other fans were exultant, but I was devastated. I wished I'd never gone to the concert.

Keith asked me what was wrong. At the time he had no idea of my ulterior motives for being there. Later I told him the whole story.

"...so now you probably think I'm a crazy lady..."

"No. I believe you, it all makes sense."

At the time I couldn't understand why Keith took it all so calmly, and why he believed me so easily, but later on it all fell into place. It was months later before Keith and I really understood his role in the story, and why he had believed me instantly. One night he had a nightmare. Its intensity has lived with him ever since, just like my dreams of the past. You can always tell a real past life memory from a dream or nightmare, because with a memory-induced dream the emotions stay with you forever. If you have a nightmare, then normally the emotions and the tears fade when you're back in the waking world. With a rekindled memory, or as in Keith's case a soul-level past life healing, they're back forever.

In Keith's dream he was in Nashville. Keith's a country singer and songwriter himself, and he'd always been very drawn to Garth, so dreaming of going to Nashville to see him wasn't too far-fetched. But the scenario that followed was very strange. In the dream Keith had seen that Garth was advertising some hay for sale, and so, thinking that was a good way to meet him, Keith decided to buy it even though he had no use for it. He found himself walking down the street with Garth, and Garth's reaction to him was very strange and out of character. He chastised Keith, saying that he'd only pretended to want to buy the item so that he could get closer to Garth. While this was true, Garth's powerful and antagonistic attitude in the dream was way over the top.

Keith got very upset, in fact he said he started to cry, which was also an exaggerated reaction to what was going on. Garth went into a store and Keith waited outside, full of anxiety. When Garth came out they stood toe to toe, staring into each other's eyes. Keith said that Garth's eyes suddenly changed into Ryan's, and Keith said he knew for sure that he was standing in front of not Garth, but Ryan.

Ryan's eyes showed the compassion that Garth's hadn't been able to, and he spoke the words that Keith believed he'd been waiting hundreds of years to hear, "I forgive you."

Whenever Keith recounts this dream, his eyes fill with tears and anyone can tell how much it meant for him to have Ryan's forgiveness. Why did he need it?

He needed forgiveness because he had been Ryan's half-brother Gerald. Since he had the dream, things have changed enormously for Keith. He's been through some necessary personal trauma, which freed him to take up the life he was meant to. He's had to struggle to get where he was meant to be, but as I write this he stands on the edge of his dream, a West End Musical, with his name on it. The musical is his master plan, what he came here to do. He made a contract with himself to bring the story to the stage, and he's going to make it.

I came to understand, a long while afterwards, that the trip to the concert hadn't been for me or Madeleine to see Garth; it had been for us both to meet Keith. God works in wondrous and mysterious ways all right, and often you can look back, like I did then, and see the jigsaw puzzle pieces slotting into place. The trip to Ireland did have another more personal purpose though. Garth had wrought another miracle in me. The pain I'd had in my stomach had gone, as if it had never been, just because I'd been in the same space as Ryan. This pain had been what I'd carried through to this life, through guilt of where he was run through with the sword, because of loving me. My pain was in the same place that the sword had struck Ryan, and now it was gone. So, some good *had* come out of it. Tony was empathic about the latest emotional see-saw I'd been subjected to, but of course he was as relieved as I was that my pain had finally gone.

Like I said, I have met many other people from that lifetime. Good people and not so good people. Is Margaret back in either of our lives? Yes, I believe so. Unfortunately, unlike Gerald, this person does not seem to have come here ready to ask forgiveness, but is instead still intent on causing mischief. Sadly, we don't all wake up to our real selves, which is of course one of our main reasons for coming here. People who don't wake up, even when given strong 'nudges', don't remember who they were and don't remember the plan they came here with. This is a vital thing to do, because it's the only way we can find real, independent happiness.

CHAPTER
TWENTY-FIVE

After some discussion, Tony and I decided to pay a visit to the house in Hambledon where the de Ports used to live. I'd named it in one hypnosis session, and I was confident I could find it. It had only been a little over 350 years since I was last there after all! I was both nervous and excited at the prospect of seeing the house again. I wasn't sure how overwhelming the memories might prove. As it happened though, I needn't have worried. I was fairly calm and apart from one very weird moment, I felt OK about being there. I was kind of switched off emotionally, and I think whoever arranged that knew exactly what they were doing!

We passed a sign for the village of Hambledon and Tony was getting a little twitchy, "You're absolutely sure this is a good idea?

"It'll be OK Tone…anyway how could I not come here, after finding out where they lived?"

At first I *couldn't* find it. We stopped in the village shop and asked where the house was. They didn't know. We stood in the main street for a while, and then I realised, *I did know!* I stopped trying to use my logical mind and let my subconscious take over. We got back into the car and headed out of the village in the direction my intuition told me to go, which was north-east. A mile or so later, and there it was on the left-hand side. I'm sure most people would call it a beautiful house, and aesthetically speaking, it is. But for me the memories overshadowed any physical attraction, and to me it was dark. On the brightest day, there would still be shadows for me there, and even if they were only shadows of the past, it would still make me shudder.

It had changed. The gothic black leaded windows and the oak, iron-studded, door had been changed for white Georgian style windows and portico. There was no name up outside, but there was no mistaking the tower extension on the right flank, or the incredibly creepy feeling the long narrow first floor window gave me, like someone had stepped on my grave. That was the window Madeleine had broken in her attempts to escape from her prison room, as Ryan was taken away.

We got out of the car and walked up the drive. I was very distracted, and kept pointing out differences I could see to Tony, like the fact that the garden wall, although it looked old, couldn't have been, as it was in the wrong place. The driveway used to be longer and grander too.

I was all for exploring, but Tony walked to the front door and knocked.

"What are you doing?" I asked him.

"Well we can't just march around the house without saying something."

"Oh, I suppose not." I joined him at the door. A lady opened it. This was the point at which I suddenly realised I didn't know what to say. The lady was getting on in years and might not take kindly to me blurting out that I used to live there in the 1600s! I found myself waffling, so she probably thought I was mad.

"Um…we think our ancestors might have lived here…is this **** House?" (The name is known but has been withheld to protect the current occupiers' privacy).

"What was their name?" she asked.

"In a stupid moment of what I'm sure was Madeleine-induced confusion I blurted out, 'Beresford'." Margaret's maiden name! Then inexplicably I asked her, "Have you found the secret room yet?" I'd had no idea I was going to say that!

She looked at me astounded, "How could you know...?"

Tony saved the day, "We have old diaries..." Now we were both trapped in a web of deceit!

Tony has a way of disarming old ladies, he always has had. He said, smiling, "Would you be kind enough to let us have a look around? He added quickly, as she again looked shocked, "Just from the outside of course." By now she probably thought we were burglars casing the joint, but she nodded that it would be OK.

"Could we take a photo or two?" Tony enquired.

"I suppose so," she agreed, staring at us as if we were either quite mad, or definitely criminals, and then she slowly closed the door. We could tell that she was still watching us though, and I can't say I blamed her. Tony took a couple of photos of the front, making sure he got the long window in one of them.

I was irresistibly drawn to the back of the house, to the barn, *his* barn.

"Jen! You can't...!" Tony protested, but at that moment, the back door opened and the lady's husband came out. It was my turn to try the old charm offensive. He was a very sweet man and was happy to allow me to look at the tithe barn. I'm sure he'd had plenty of requests over the years. It was of historic interest after all.

I walked slowly over to it. Tony followed me and stood at the open door. I was transfixed. I peered into the shadowy interior.

The atmosphere in there was almost overwhelming. It was

smaller than I expected. It was also as if the place was haunted. I could almost *see* Ryan sitting in the shadows. I walked further into the barn and sat on a pile of logs in one corner. I reached out my hand, but of course there was nobody there, even though I couldn't help feeling a presence. I got up and went back to Tony, where he stood in the doorway. My eyes had mysteriously misted over, and I wiped them. I blew a slow and gentle kiss to the inside of the barn, while emotions and passions whirled through my mind, and then I turned to look at the house.

At the back the windows were still the originals, black diamond leaded glass. In the roof at the back was a gable window, and that too filled me with inexplicable trepidation. It had to be the one Madeleine jumped from. The dairy had been turned into a modern bungalow, so I was very glad that at least Ryan's old barn was still there. I was quite pleased that I remained conveniently, and mysteriously, 'switched off' for the whole visit, apart from the brief moment in the barn.

It was to be entirely different at the church.

One very good thing came of that visit to the house. I believe that while I was there I 'collected' a fragment of my soul that had been left there all those years before, when Madeleine had died. This tiny facet was vital for me to be able to feel like a complete person. I regained self-confidence from that reunion, and my character became stronger. I became more courageous. I wonder today whether ghosts could actually be fragments of *us*, left behind after a past life trauma, waiting for us to come and collect them.

Tony and I decided that we should visit the church were Ryan and Madeleine were married. We'd been puzzled when looking at the map, because the only village with an abbey church that we could find within possible riding distance from the house at Hambledon, was called Milton Abbas. There was no Middleton, which was what I said it was called. We drove to the village of Milton Abbas. When we drove through the main street, I told Tony that it looked all wrong and couldn't be the right village. First of all, the village itself should have been around the Abbey, close in to its protective walls, whereas this village was about a quarter of a mile from the church. Also it ran along both sides of one main street and there was little else there, but back in 1638 it was a complex cluster of dwellings, all mixed together in a jumble. Some houses, hovels really, were back-to-back, with a tangle of paths and animal pens in between. The cottages looked as if they dated from the right period, but they were definitely all laid out wrongly.

But there was no mistaking the church itself. It lies in a wooded bowl, and looks almost as if it grew there naturally. When I turned the latch and went in, it was like entering another world. Tony said that going up the aisle to the altar was something I should do alone, and so I walked by myself up the aisle, and stood where I had as Madeleine all those years ago. The altar area, as I'd remembered, is highly carved of stone, from floor to ceiling. The most amazing thing of all concerns my memory of the semi-circle of candles around the altar. For in the carved stone wall, at intervals of about a foot, there are candle sconces. And on the day we were at the church, for some inexplicable reason, there were actually candles burning in the sconces, just as there had been on Ryan and Madeleine's wedding day. I've never seen this feature in any other church.

My emotions in this place were unchecked, and I couldn't help tears pouring down my cheeks as I stood there. On one level, I could feel Ryan's presence next to me, shoulder to shoulder with me, but on another level, I felt so alone because he wasn't really there. After a while Tony joined me and I clung to him gratefully, knowing that in this life I was with the *right* soul mate. It was a wonderful place and I will never forget it. When Tony joined me, he told me he'd made an amazing find. At the side of the church there was a painting depicting the village in the mid 1600s. It was exactly as I had pictured and described it, and what's more, before it was burnt down in the late 1600s, it had been called Middleton.

I just had to go to America to meet Garth and close things. It was obviously the only way.

Tony tried to reassure me, "Flying *is* safe. You've more chance of being struck by lightning tomorrow than of being involved in a plane crash."

It took quite a while to absorb enough of Madeleine's courage, but she wouldn't let it rest, so finally in 1999 I decided I could do it. To Tony's complete incredulity, I booked us both on a holiday to Nashville. Also accompanying us was Jared, Ryan's friend from the 17th century. Of course in this life he wasn't called Jared, but Graham, and this time he wasn't gay. We had made contact with Graham through a series of synchronistic events, and he, like Keith, had immediately recognized Madeleine and Ryan's story on a soul level. Under hypnotic regression, he came to understand that by the time Jared was able to return to Hambledon, after two years absence, Ryan was gone and Madeleine was dead. Having failed in his promise to Ryan to take care of Madeleine in that life, he was now determined to do it this time. This time his promise included helping get Madeleine back to Ryan. Graham and I are almost complete opposites, and yet there is a bond between us that is stronger than time.

While the countdown seemed to take forever, when the day to leave finally came it seemed to arrive in a rush. Before I knew it we were packed, in the car, and on our way to the airport. I couldn't believe that I was actually going to get on a plane! It was only 5am but, believe me, I was well awake! Passing through airport security was interesting, speaking as one who has never been admitted through those mysterious portals before. Before I knew it we were at the bottom of the aircraft steps. Just to add difficulty to my nervous condition, we were flying to a major airport, Amsterdam, from our local one. This meant no concealing tunnels and no pretending it was a bus! No; we had actually to walk out across the tarmac and up steps into the plane. I tried hard not to study all the bolts and rivets and just *trust* that the wings were securely fixed on to the body of the plane!

The plane itself looked too big to ever get off the ground and yet too small to be safe. It was also a propeller plane, not a jet. By then I just thought, oh well, it's too late to worry about it. I went up the steps ahead of Tony, and a mischievous part of me made me turn round to him and smile broadly into his anxious face. I know that up to then Tony had still had his doubts as to whether or not I'd be able to do it at all, therefore his expression when I smiled at him was hilarious.

I *was* scared. But I took a deep breath, remembering what Ryan and Madeleine had gone through to be together, and in I went. As I sat down I felt the terrified part of me receding into some small safe place in the centre of my being. Madeleine was taking over, as I'd known she would. It was surprisingly small inside the plane but more comfortable than I'd imagined.

As we taxied down to the end of the runway, my heart was rising into my throat, and then as we trembled with the planes engines as the power went on, I didn't know whether to laugh or cry. What was I doing there? When it took off I actually enjoyed it. I've never been one for fairground rides but I enjoyed the power of the aircraft. The only moment of take-off that took my breath away was when we reached our correct altitude. At that point some power comes off, the aircraft seems to slow down and you wonder if it's going to stay up there as it drops slightly beneath you!

Landing was interesting. I wasn't able to look out of the window at first because it made me dizzy, but by the time we approached Amsterdam I was brave enough. The closer we got to the ground the safer I felt. I know that was illogical, but I did. I resisted the impulse to kiss the ground when we got off the plane. It was rather worrying to have to land and take off again, not only in Amsterdam, but also again in Detroit, but we made it. On the flight between Amsterdam and Detroit we did experience some turbulence. At this time I retreated into the past and believed myself to be traveling along a road in a bumpy horse and cart, which helped a lot.

Hours and hours later we were finally driving through the streets of Nashville. Finally, really there, it was hard to believe. I called Garth's office to ask if he was there. They said he wasn't, but I think they were intrigued as they asked me to go and meet his manager and attorney. It was…interesting. I soon discovered where they were 'coming from', when the attorney asked me, "So if Garth admitted this was all true, would you consider him to be your husband?"

Ah, bless them, they thought I was after his money, that I was going to set a legal precedent to claim alimony from a past life marriage! I explained that they were being a little silly, that the best husband in the world was waiting for me in the car park, and that they had nothing to worry about on that score. It seemed to settle them down.

Having been convinced that they had no worries about my intentions financially, they also accepted that I was sincere in my beliefs, which was nice. But, they told me that Garth was in Los Angeles for an award ceremony, and that he wasn't expected back until after I was planning on going home. I was very upset, as you can imagine. After fighting phobias, and braving my worst fears, I was going to miss him. It seemed like it was never going to happen.

20 May 1640 was the last day Madeleine saw Ryan. In May 1997 I saw Garth live in concert, and now it was May 1999. If I'd considered this, I wouldn't have been so surprised when on the afternoon of 3rd May I was overwhelmed with the sudden knowledge that Garth was not in Los Angeles; indeed he was right there in Nashville, despite what everyone thought. In just the same way that Ryan and Madeleine had known a spiritual link with each other, so my soul had sensed that Garth's soul was nearby.

Magic was in the air, and it was all perfect. Garth responded to a message and came to meet us. It was Ryan and Madeleine's moment. My heart was filled with total, satisfied joy. I'd done it! As he stepped towards me, and I stepped towards him, our outstretched hands met, touched, grasped. This time the two hands were solid. I looked into his eyes, and deep inside I could see Ryan.

I was swept away into the past, or was it the present?

The sword pierced Ryan's body as he was helpless on the ground. The swordsman let go of the sword and Ryan rolled away, blood spurting from his back, where the blade had emerged. As Ryan reached out to someone unseen, the kilted warrior leaned down to take the ring from his hand.

Madeleine stepped into view. She grabbed Ryan's hand. A sword plunged into her back and she fell into Ryan's arms. As their blood mingled, I was drawn back to this life and to a road in Nashville. I was staring into a pair of wide blue eyes. His eyes were lit up, as if powered from within by an unimaginable force.

Garth pulled me into his arms and hugged me, so tight I could hardly breathe.

It was over.

The circle was closed.

CHAPTER TWENTY-SIX

S o, does everyone have past lives? Over the years since this all happened I have learned a great deal about the subject. Yes, we all do, and the average number, for someone who has reached the stage of being spiritually aware enough to consider the subject, is eighty-five lives. Our past lives do always affect our current ones too. How could they not?

Tony and I often reminisce about all the changes and amazing things that have happened to us. There are so many things to think about. Tony for instance trained to become a spiritual healer, and is proving to be very powerful at channelling Universal energy, and at being able to heal people in distant countries without ever having met them. This is yet another off-shoot of the 'ripples' effect.

We've heard of many couples whose marriage actually fell apart when just one of them developed spiritually. It seems to happen a lot, sadly. Tony and I have been fated to grow spiritually together. We've become ever closer as a result of it. A good friend of mine told me that she thinks Tony is the only person who could have been married to me in this life, because he is the only person in the world who could have accepted, and seen me through all this change. I'm inclined to agree with her.

He continues to be my best friend, my lover, my soul mate, and the best man I have ever known. For a while I was a newspaper columnist. This involved my writing a regular article on alternative therapies, which also involved me trying them all out too - very interesting.

I've become a moderately successful song writer, and my 'best' performance so far has been a song called 'I'm Still Falling', which was inspired by Ryan's words to Madeleine, and was featured on an album, earning the singer, Barry Upton, a Silver Disc. I also co-wrote the theme song for a TV show.

The most amazing thing for me was probably the materialisation of my own TV show. Who would have thought it? Who would have thought that sad person I used to be could have changed so much, into someone capable of doing all this? Not me. This programme went out live, five days a week, and allowed me to interview all kinds of alternative people, and discuss all kinds of alternative subjects, from reflexology to witchcraft, from alternative weddings to UFOs, and anything else I found interesting. It was my classroom.

It's heart warming to realise that there is so much interest in spiritual matters now. And that people are becoming more open towards the beliefs of others. I'm certain it's the way to world peace. We need to embrace our differences and not try to bend others and change them into us.

I heard a story the other day. It was about a herd of antelopes that had been brought into captivity, albeit for justifiable reasons. As the keepers watched, a herd of elephants wandered up and surrounded the pen. The matriarch of the elephant herd opened the gate latch with her trunk, and pulled the gate open. All the antelopes ran to freedom. The elephants did this without once trying to turn the antelopes into elephants.

This book wasn't meant to convince anyone that past lives are real, or to tell them that they must believe in any one thing. It was to share an extraordinary experience I had with anyone who wanted to share it. It was to tell anyone contemplating suicide, if you turn your back on your tomorrow, you never know what you might miss - look what I would have missed! To show anyone living with depression, that a life, anyone's life, can change in an instant.

It was to put the record straight and to tell the world what Margaret and Edwin did to Ryan Fitzgerald. Their unreasoning vindictiveness and cruelty amazes me still.

Maybe it'll show Garth something about himself.

I hope that my ripples might plant a tiny seed of spirituality in some people. Not necessarily the seed of reincarnation and karma, but *any* tiny seed of spiritual awareness. Awareness that the material world we struggle in is not the be all and end all some people think it is. It will hopefully show people that there are more important things to worry about than having the best car, best house or best furniture that some devote their whole lives to. That real violence is not glamorous, but is dirty and horrendous. To show that love IS real, and that it endures and can overcome all odds.

It was to allow me to be a very tiny cog in a gigantic wheel of world awakening.

It's a story of love for lovers, a story of romance for romantics, it's a story of openheartedness for those with open hearts, and a story of spirituality for those who believe there is more to life than we know.

I was guided onto my true path by a second angel encounter. It was on a train, of all places. Deep in meditation I found myself in the presence of a huge golden being. Words cannot describe the unconditional and unique love that one receives from, and gives to, an angel. I came to realise that this was a 'past life angel' or 'soul angel', which had helped to 'wake me up' and would now show me my master plan. These angels nudge us to remember our past, because this is the best way for us to understand what and who we really are. It enables us to get messages, like I did, to show us what we came here to do. My 'master plan' is to be a seed-planter, and I have been blessed with many tools to do my work. I literally am meant to plant a seed of spiritual awareness in people. It's as simple, and as beautiful, as that.

When I look back now at what was obviously angelic intervention, from that very first message to switch on the TV, I wonder how I ever used to survive without communicating with angels. I suppose I almost didn't survive. Everyone can talk to his or her own angels; they just have to ask. Now angels are with me every day, everywhere, and now that I know it, I never feel alone.

Garth Brooks has changed remarkably in many ways since we met too. He decided to retire from the music business and concentrate on being a father to his children. You will know by now that I'm not a great believer in coincidences being just that, and therefore the following 'coincidences' are synchronicities, and are very valid to me.

Garth invented the character of Chris Gaines, and made a 'rock' album under that name, at around the same time I was writing my first book on the subject of my past life. The press ridiculed Garth for his invention because they couldn't understand why a fictional character seemed so important to him, and why he felt the need to go to the extremes of dressing up as a character that was essentially supposed to be created for a film role. The rock album that 'Chris Gaines' made was superb, and yet the media made sure it didn't succeed as it should have done, concentrating on Garth's need to wear a long wig when singing as Gaines, rather than the quality of the music.

In Numerology terms the fictitious birth date of Gaines that Garth invented, and the factual birth date of Ryan, add up to the same base number.

The two names, Chris Gaines and Ryan Fitzgerald have the same numerical value. So taking these two facts into account, could it be possible that Garth's 'invention' of Gaines was actually a manifestation, albeit unconsciously, of his past life as Ryan?

When the Chris Gaines' CD finally appeared, the cover photo was a revelation to me. The man on the cover *was* Garth, and yet he *wasn't*. The face on the cover was much thinner than Garth's, younger, and dangerous looking, with long, shaggy black hair, his blue eyes peering through it. He matched my description of Ryan perfectly.

I was told quite recently that Garth has a scar, which corresponds exactly to where Ryan was stabbed. Garth got the scar in a road accident, and in his words a long piece of metal broke off the car body, and he was 'skewered'. Could that piece of metal be the 20th Century version of a sword? And he got the injury at almost the same age Ryan was when he died from his.

When I visited Hambledon, I was able to identify the house, the priest's hole within it, the green lane, pubs that are no longer pubs, such as The Green Man, and of course the changes in the village of Middleton and the church. I was also able to identify that there had once been an inn up the High Street of Hambledon, and that the cottages opposite the Old George had once been different to how they are today. Apparently they were burnt down, and rebuilt in the 18th century. I called the town Hamledune, under hypnosis, which was the correct pronunciation in the 17th Century. I identified various people, families and estates of the time, with unusual names, such as Chalfont and Symons and Capjohn.

Garth is reputed to have a dread of deep water, just as Ryan did. He is, not surprisingly, said to be alarmed at the sight of his own blood.

You have read the account of the forest fire which Ryan helped fight, and which started at a neighbour's property. In Oklahoma a few years ago, Garth helped to fight a grass fire, which started at his neighbour's property, and he saved a boy called...Ryan.

This is the report of the incident...

OCTOBER 21 — COLLINSVILLE, OK: Garth Brooks has several new fans in Oklahoma. And he's pretty much a superhero in the eyes of Kevin and Jodi Cooper after evacuating their two sons from the path of a grass fire southeast of Collinsville on Thursday. The Tulsa World reported that the two boys were home alone on fall break from school Thursday when Garth Brooks and another man began beating on the door of their wood-frame house. "I opened the door and the guy said, 'There's a fire. You've got to get out,' so I went out," said 10-year-old Randall. "The guy who turned out to be Garth was back behind him. I was yelling back at the house, 'Ryan, there's a fire!'"

Ryan, 14, was taking a shower and didn't hear his brother's calls, but he did hear Brooks, who has relatives in the area. "He was yelling, 'Ryan, Ryan!' I was like, 'Who are you?' and he said, 'Get in the truck.'" Brooks drove Ryan through dense smoke to a neighbor's truck, where he joined his brother. As reported in The Tulsa World.

It appears then that we're sometimes fated to re-live permutations of the same events, sometimes in an attempt to make us remember the scenario from the past that was similar. Sometimes so that each time we reach a higher plane, until we are ready to go on to wherever we are meant to reach. Upward spiralling circles…started by ripples?

Joan Cook was the first person in Garth's management offices to read the story. She has known Garth for many years. Her response was that she believed Garth was Ryan, because they are *so* alike. Her words were, "You've never even met him (Garth), and yet you know him in a much deeper way than a lot of people who have known him for years. Everything Ryan says or does is exactly what Garth would do in the same circumstances."

It's fascinating that a lot of the songs that Garth has co-written, or chosen to record since I wrote this story down, have seemed to match parts of it, or feelings from it, so well. It could possibly be perhaps that certain words trigger emotional responses from that lifetime, which influence choices and assist creative output. Many singer/songwriters have said that their inspiration for songs comes from 'out there somewhere'. Garth recently recorded a song he wrote back in 2000, about reincarnation.

Imagine my surprise when Garth brought out the song, 'Ireland', a complete departure from his usual style. The song talks about a young Irishman, fighting and dying in a strange land.

The story goes on…forever…
Your mind holds the power. Your heart holds the desire.
Your soul holds the key.
You just need the courage to turn it.

O

is a symbol of the world,
of oneness and unity. O Books
explores the many paths of wholeness
and spiritual understanding which
different traditions have developed down
the ages. It aims to bring this knowledge
in accessible form, to a general readership,
providing practical spirituality to today's seekers.

For the full list of over 200 titles covering:

- CHILDREN'S PRAYER, NOVELTY AND GIFT BOOKS
- CHILDREN'S CHRISTIAN AND SPIRITUALITY
- CHRISTMAS AND EASTER
- RELIGION/PHILOSOPHY
- SCHOOL TITLES
- ANGELS/CHANNELLING
- HEALING/MEDITATION
- SELF-HELP/RELATIONSHIPS
- ASTROLOGY/NUMEROLOGY
- SPIRITUAL ENQUIRY
- CHRISTIANITY, EVANGELICAL
  AND LIBERAL/RADICAL
- CURRENT AFFAIRS
- HISTORY/BIOGRAPHY
- INSPIRATIONAL/DEVOTIONAL
- WORLD RELIGIONS/INTERFAITH
- BIOGRAPHY AND FICTION
- BIBLE AND REFERENCE
- SCIENCE/PSYCHOLOGY

Please visit our website,
www.O-books.net